the best of

HAWAI'I

wedding book

A Guide to
Maui, Lana'i, and Kaua'i

the best of

HAWAI'I

wedding book

Top Locations, Services,

and Resources for Your

Destination Wedding

TAMMY ASH PERKINS

INNER OCEAN PUBLISHING
Maui • San Francisco

Inner Ocean Publishing, Inc.
P.O. Box 1239
Makawao, Maui, HI 96768-1239
www.innerocean.com

Cover and book design by Laura Beers

Inner Ocean Publishing is a member of Green Press Initiative, a nonprofit program dedicated to supporting publishers in their efforts to reduce their use of fiber sourced from endangered forests. We elected to print this title on 50% postconsumer recycled paper with the recycled portion processed chlorine free.

As a result, we have saved the following resources: 33 trees, 1,557 lbs of solid waste, 14,120 gallons of water, 3,058 lbs of net greenhouse gases, 5,679 kw hours of electricity.

For more information on the Green Press Initiative, visit www.greenpressinitiative.org.

PUBLISHER CATALOGING-IN-PUBLICATION DATA

Perkins, Tammy.
The best of Hawai'i wedding book : a guide to Maui, Lana'i, and
Kaua'i : top locations, services, and resources for your destination
wedding / Tammy Perkins. — Maui : Inner Ocean, 2006.
p. ; cm.
ISBN-13: 978-1-930722-64-4 (pbk.)
ISBN-10: 1-930722-64-8 (pbk.)
Includes index.
1. Destination weddings—Hawaii. 2. Destination weddings—
Hawaii—Guidebooks. 3. Weddings—Planning. I. Title.
HQ745 .P47 2006
395.2/2—dc22 0603

Printed in the United States of America

05 06 07 08 09 10 DATA 10 9 8 7 6 5 4 3 2 1

DISTRIBUTED BY PUBLISHER'S GROUP WEST
For information on promotions, bulk purchases, premiums, or educational use, please contact:
866.731.2216 or sales@innerocean.com.

Disclaimer: We have made every effort to make this book as accurate as possible at the time of publication. Prices and facilities are subject to change. Please contact locations and vendors to confirm information found in this book.

TABLE OF CONTENTS

introduction

When I started my wedding business more than twelve years ago, destination weddings were just starting to become popular. I remember a couple dressed in traditional wedding attire hiring a "bird man" to bring in and strategically place several parrots and tropical birds on their shoulders, arms, and even their heads, all just to get the perfect tropical-themed photograph. Working in video production at the time, I got to know everyone in the business and every wedding location available. I discovered how different a "traditional" wedding in Hawai'i often is and how amazing a Hawaiian-themed wedding can be. And most important, I learned how to serve the destination client.

With all the research I conducted, all the weddings I experienced, and everything I learned (together with my "keen eye"), I developed a growing urge to provide couples with the opportunity to experience the best of what Hawai'i has to offer on one of the most incredible days of their lives. The pure romance of the occasion inspired me so much so that I started a company and vowed to be the leader in the industry by constantly setting the standard. Now, twelve years later, dresses have changed, hairstyles have changed, colors have changed, trends have changed—yet there is one thing that remains the same: Couples hunger for something special, fun, and exciting. They crave to have a wedding designed to be a reflection of who they are. More than anything else, they want a wedding that is more intimate and memorable than the traditional wedding back home. With more and more brides catching on to this trend, Hawai'i has grown into one of the world's premier wedding destinations. After all, why not? It has everything a destination bride could ever dream of, and more.

More than twenty thousand wedding ceremonies are conducted each year in Hawai'i, so it was astonishing to me that there was no accurate information about Hawai'i to read, carry around, and share with family and friends. After scouring many wedding books, bridal guides, wedding planners, and countless magazines, I realized that not one of them had been written by anyone with experience in the field. From flowers to venues to vendors, there is no "typical" wedding when you marry in Hawai'i, and most importantly, a very different set of rules apply when you're planning a destination wedding.

This book was created to guide you through the variety of choices you will have to make when planning your destination wedding. With so many choices the Islands have to offer, I have taken careful consideration in providing you with the best locations, top vendors, and the best professional services, which I hope will take the guesswork out of planning. Whether you choose to plan your own destination wedding or opt to hire a consultant, you will have the most updated information for the entire process. This resource ultimately allows you to sleep easy, knowing that your wedding will be everything that you've wanted it to be.

I have planned thousands of weddings, from the most glorious celebrity weddings to the most private, intimate affairs. Working with destination brides from all over the world, I have been the eyes and ears for many who have not even set foot in Hawai'i until their wedding festivities begin. It is my hope that this guide will provide brides, grooms, mothers of brides, and any other interested parties with the essential information needed for getting married on Maui, Lana'i, or Kaua'i.

How to Use This Guide

Each section of this book offers all the little details to help you make the best wedding decisions. I encourage you to flag, underline, and write notes throughout this book. Have it handy as you talk to family members, potential planners, and vendors.

Part 1 provides general information about marrying in Hawai'i, including marriage requirements and weather considerations, and also specific information about Maui, Kaua'i, and Lana'i so you can decide which island fits you best. This section is a great place to start to determine if Hawai'i is the wedding destination for you. The Hawai'i Visitors Bureau also has a great Web site at www.gohawaii.com. The other sections can be navigated as you wish, depending on what you'd like to dive into first. As Maui has the most resources, I offer reviews and listings for Maui first, followed by selections in Kaua'i, and then Lana'i.

In part 2, you will discover the beauty of the top wedding locations on these islands, with descriptive information to feed your imagination, and important details regarding each venue so that you're not surprised when you arrive. The color insert found in the book showcases photography of a selection of the locations, and I recommend visiting the websites listed in the book for further review. Each type of site has an introduction with general information and summaries of things to consider prior to finalizing your decision. There are also suggestions for nearby dining options, many of which are detailed in the Restaurant Section of the book, or find contact information in the resaurant listings. You may want to breeze through this section and tag the ones that strike you most, and then read the nitty-gritty details of your favorites.

Part 3 contains valuable information about professional services ranging from officiants to florists, plus handy listings. Get the inside scoop on licensing requirements, fees, and vendor guidelines specific to our islands, which aren't publicly displayed anywhere else. More so than for standard weddings, travel and accommodation information is essential for the destination wedding. You will find these resources in part 4.

In my experience, I've found that brides often don't realize how different planning a destination wedding is, so I've created a planner to supplement any other tools you may be using. In part 5 you will find worksheets plus many tips on making your day run smoothly. Fill out the destination planner worksheet with the key points of your dream wedding so that you can get a better handle on your vision. Part 5 also outlines the benefits of enlisting the help of a professional planner. If you decide to hire a planner, then you will need to start interviewing companies so that you can secure their services right away. Your wedding coordinator immediately begins to work as an extension of you and can start by providing you with necessary information on locations that match your preferences. If you decide to be your own wedding planner, parts 2 and 3 will provide you with a solid base. You can then refer to the detailed timeline at the back of the book to guide you further. Following these simple steps will help you with the entire planning process and ensure the success of your destination wedding.

Currently, same-sex marriages are not legalized in the state of Hawai'i. However, many couples hold commitment ceremonies. In general, all the same resources apply, yet not all professionals support it. I suggest that you verify the prospective vendor's position prior to hiring them.

If you have the opportunity to visit the island prior to securing any services, please be aware that visiting prospective venues during an actual event is almost unheard of. References are not available for a venue itself, although they will be available for vendors and planners. Also, if you want to investigate the vendors' services (attending music rehearsals, requesting floral samples, tasting cakes, and so on), you will have to pay regular rates to do so.

Several of these reputable vendors do not have Web sites, professional demos, or official contracts. Why? Because they have enough business through wedding planners, resorts, and referrals that they simply don't need to advertise. They often are so busy that they turn away jobs. This is why booking early and finding someone you can trust to help you with your selections are important. So, close your eyes and start fantasizing with your love about the most special day of your lives. The magic of the islands awaits you.

The vendor listings are the best of what Maui, Kaua'i, and Lana'i have to offer. Inclusion in this book is based on good business ethics, working relationships, the ability to consistently deliver a quality product, the level of skill, experience in the field, and most important, the ability to deliver outstanding customer service.

© Mike Sydney

Choosing a Destination Wedding in Hawai'i

Destination weddings are one of the most popular ways for the modern bride to get married. Choosing to marry in a faraway location allows you to create an unforgettable ceremony for you and your guests, as well as an opportunity to show off your adventurous spirit. It's a surprise to many brides that destination weddings can cost less than a regular wedding, but traveling to a destination location does minimize the guest list and combines the honeymoon and wedding all in one trip.

Hawaiian-themed weddings offer a flair all their own. One of my most memorable weddings was held at Po'olenalena Beach, where the seated guests were captivated by the beauty of the coastline as they were serenaded by the sounds of the waves and calmed by the ocean breeze. In the company of a royal Polynesian court, a resident musician beat a deep native rhythm on Tongan drums to kick off the processional. Colorful kahili bearers dressed in tropically patterned sarongs marched down the aisle and positioned themselves on each side of the outdoor altar. You could hear the sounds of a conch shell resonate across the beach as the blower approached and then made his way down the aisle. Immediately following him marched a Hawaiian chanter reciting the traditional blessings, with two maidens carrying beautifully lit torches following close behind. The air was filled with fragrant plumeria blossoms as the majestic vision of the bride coming down the aisle took the guests' breath away. Immediately following the ceremony, the processional released a loud song in the form of a fast Tahitian-style celebration dance. The dance served as a consummation of the ceremony and blessing for the couple as they shared their first married moments together.

But getting married in Hawai'i doesn't mean you have to incorporate local culture into your ceremony. The setting of sand, sun, and gorgeous flowers can make any wedding brilliant. There is something about the traditional attire in a tropical setting that will make your wedding stand apart from all others. So even if you choose to go the traditional route, the beauty of Hawai'i naturally sets the mood and makes a perfect venue for your special day.

WHY HAWAI'I

Location

Hawai'i is exceptionally beautiful, and there is no better way to say "I do" than in one of the most romantic, and remote places on earth. From the relaxed lifestyle to the spirit of aloha, Hawai'i welcomes complete strangers with open arms, making you feel right at home. Also, Hawai'i is a world-class destination, so the islands are accustomed to delivering remarkable hospitality. It's simply paradise.

Climate

The climate in Hawai'i has consistently comfortable temperatures, so choosing an indoor or outdoor setting for your wedding makes it possible any month of the year. The cool tropical breezes and the fresh air delight your senses from the moment you step off the plane.

Culture

Stories of old Hawai'i, its kings and queens, princesses, and warriors are carried on in the community today through its music, dance, and ancient traditions, making this place unlike any other place on the planet. The Islands' way of life simply melts all your concerns away as you discover new colors in the rainbow, taste the exotic flavors of local cuisine, enjoy the fragrant scents of a tuberose blossom, swim with a rare sea turtle, or learn how to completely chill while listening to the sounds of the Pacific Ocean. Hawai'i's culture offers you an unlimited number of new experiences, just waiting for you to explore.

Creativity

A wedding in Hawai'i can be a complete expression of who you are, and you have many resources available to you. If you're artistic, then a basket weaver, lei maker, or wood carver can be added to the occasion. If you're adventurous, then select from a variety of remote locations that express your inner explorer. And if you're just looking for that Island flair, then there's nothing like a having a Hawaiian-themed wedding. Suggestions can be found in the Destination Planner. The options are limitless.

ABOUT MAUI, KAUA'I, AND LANA'I

The island of **Maui** first emerged from the sea millions of years ago, when volcanic eruptions formed two islands that were later joined by an enormous lava flow that filled the gap between them. As the eruptions ceased and the volcanoes known as the West Maui Mountains and Haleakala (House of the Sun) went dormant, Maui was left with rich red soil. Ideal for growing sugarcane and pineapple, Maui's landscape varies widely, from palm-fringed beaches with gorgeous waterfalls and rugged sea cliffs to the vast reaches of Haleakala's moonlike crater and mist-enveloped forests. The legacy of the volcanoes is matched only by the bottomless mysteries of the Pacific. Its reefs teem with tropical fish, dolphins, sea turtles, and whales, and temperatures range from 70 to 80 degrees Fahrenheit.

With its endless natural beauty and friendly people overflowing with the aloha spirit, Maui sets itself apart from the other islands by the variety of excursions it offers everyone—shopping, kite surfing, kayaking, hiking, or just lounging on the beach. You can take a scenic drive around the island along the road to Hana, attend a luau, snorkel or scuba dive with turtles and tropical fish, enjoy a sailing tour, or, if you're feeling adventurous, go up in a helicopter to get a glimpse of some of the most amazing waterfalls imaginable. Nothing embodies the spirit of the islands like the magic of Maui.

Kaua'i is the northernmost island in the Hawai'i chain. Here you can explore the famous Waimea Canyon, Fern Grotto, and the breathtaking Na Pali Coast. On a clear day you can see the valleys cut through the cliffs all the way down to the sea. This island is somewhat removed from civilization, so be prepared to slow down when you get here. For more information visit the Kaua'i Visitors Bureau Web site at www.kauaidiscovery.com.

The most difficult thing about visiting Kaua'i, besides getting on the plane to return home, is knowing where to start. The quiet majesty of this island's lush tropical setting and extraordinary natural heritage give you the chance to experience a taste of old Hawai'i. Away from the hustle and bustle of city life, you'll have every opportunity in the world to spend your days enjoying the sun, sand, and surf with the love of your life. With temperatures ranging from the mid-70s to mid-80s and the mountains collecting the second-greatest amount of rainfall in the world, the Garden Isle provides a perfect venue for couples in search of a thriving tropical environment.

With fewer than three thousand inhabitants, the island of **Lana'i** creates a sense of utmost seclusion. Hidden along its coastline are untouched beaches, rarely disturbed by foot traffic. While watching the royal blue waves rolling up onto the powdery white sand, the only noise that surrounds you is the whisper of the trade winds. With the grace and dignity of old Hawai'i, two luxurious resorts await you with award-winning cuisine, outstanding spa treatments, world-class golfing, and impeccable service.

Lana'i City, built in 1924, remains true to its quaint and rustic origins. Roosters still crow with the dawning of the day atop brightly painted roofs in gardens shaded by banana and papaya trees. One of the best-kept secrets in Hawai'i, Lana'i is a place that you can escape to, a world that you have only dreamed of yet never knew existed. An island all its own, a place where deer roam free and forests are filled with rare plants and flowers, Lana'i beckons to the hopeless romantic.

For more information on the Islands in general, as well as activities, shopping, local event calendars, and much more, the Hawai'i Visitors Bureau's Web site (www.gohawaii.com) is a great source of information.

Time and Weather Considerations

Believe it or not, Hawai'i has a wedding season. In general, weddings occur during the months of May through October (May and June being the busiest). When you're traveling to Hawai'i, every day is a holiday, so getting married during the week is a great option. The weekends are always busier with local crowds enjoying the best beaches and most popular locations themselves. Because we never know what nature has in store for us, there is never any guarantee it won't rain, especially during the months of December through May, with March and April being the rainiest.

Regardless of the time of year you plan on getting married, Hawai'i hosts desirable weather all year long. Summer days on most parts of Maui, Lana'i, and Kaua'i consistently bless us with temperatures in the upper 80s, while the winter months feature temperatures in the mid-70s, with some rain always falling in the most tropical areas of each island. Come rain, sun, wind, a waterfall, tropical garden, private oceanfront lawn, or the lush grounds of a resort makes for one of the most memorable wedding locations in the world.

Hawai'i's Marriage Requirements

The state of Hawai'i makes it very easy for couples to get married. Agents are strategically placed on each island, so you can choose one close to where you might be staying. Marriage licenses are issued no earlier than thirty days prior to your wedding date, brides are not required to take a rubella test, and no documents need to be obtained if you are coming from another country. The bride and groom must both be present, and your marriage license is valid anywhere in the world. A license appointment takes about fifteen minutes, and you will be asked to fill out a form (available to you prior to your arrival). The future bride and groom will then be required to present a valid photo identification such as a driver's license, along with a fee of $60 in cash (scheduled to increase in 2006). Divorce papers also must be presented if the divorce was finalized within thirty days of your wedding date. You must take your marriage license with you to the ceremony so that your minister can sign it (witnesses are optional).

After the ceremony your minister will send in your signed and completed license application to the department of health, which will take four to five months to issue you an official copy of your license. It is illegal for your minister to make a copy of the application to give to you. When you apply for your license, your agent will provide a form that you may send in with a fee if you would like to expedite this process. To obtain more information, to receive an application, or to check up on your application afterward, you can visit the Department of Health's Web site at www.hawaii.gov/doh.

LICENSERS

For a smooth experience with a marriage license agent, it is important to respect and follow the selected licenser's guidelines, including appointment times. Most licensers have offices in their homes, and all of them are open by appointment only from Monday through Saturday, 8 a.m. to 5 p.m. You must schedule your appointment in advance, be on time, bring your photo ID, and be able to pay the licensing fee in cash. Once your appointment has been scheduled, a map to the agent's office can be forwarded to you upon your request.

LICENSERS

MAUI

Althea Bongolan
45 Poniu Circle
Wailuku, HI 96793
808-244-1560

Lynn Steberg
277 Wili Ko Place, Number 232
Lahaina, HI 96761
808-667-4099

Sherilynn Takushi
181 Lahainaluna Road, Suite K
Lahaina, HI 96761
808-661-9696

Cynthia Wolfe
2561 Omiko Place
Kihei, HI 96753
808-875-8459

KAUA'I

Kawaihau District

Kenneth or Lynn Kubota
4-1300 Kuhio Highway
Kapaa, Kauai, HI 96746
808-822-7354 or 808-822-4581

Kamika Smith, Walter Smith,
and Grace Apana
174 Wailua Road
Kapaa, HI 96746
808-821-6887

Lihu'e District

Janice Bond
3920 Hunakai Street
Lihue, HI 96766
808-246-0174

Tim Mira and Dera Caberto
Office of the Governor
3060 Eiwa Street
Lihue, HI 96766
808-274-3100

Hanalei District

Dayna Santos and Jamie DeVorre
5-5161 Kuhio Highway, Suite 210
Hanalei, HI 96714
808-826-7742

Koloa District

Sandra or Alan R. Matsumoto
P.O. Box 805
Kalaheo, HI 96741
808-332-7133

LANA'I

Leticia Castillo
P.O. Box 630806
Lanai City, HI 96763
808-565-6380

© Michael Andrews

Part Two | CEREMONY AND RECEPTION SITES

© A & C Photography

beaches

beaches

With all the beauty a beach setting provides, you have endless opportunities to be creative. I have hosted some of the most romantic
beach weddings in Hawai'i, from small parties to more than a hundred people, resplendent with arches, canoe arrivals, Hawaiian blessings, wedding-
party swims, and more. Public beaches are available on a first-come, first-
served basis. They are the busiest at sunset and on holidays.
Weekday-morning weddings ensure smaller crowds and cooler weather.
There are no permit requirements for beach weddings in Hawai'i, so using
the beach as your wedding location is free—but it can be tricky. Since all
beaches are public, be prepared for some uninvited guests to be in attendance, even another wedding party.

As with any outdoor wedding, be prepared for the elements—the heat
and glare of the sun, gusty winds, and sand should be taken into account
in all your preparations. Creating your ceremony area can be challenging
since nothing can be legally blocked off. Small tents, tables, and chairs
can be set up for short periods as long as you're respectful and willing to
share your event space with the general public. Battery-operated amplified
music is also appropriate as long as you're considerate of others nearby.
Absolutely no confetti, rice, or bird seed is allowed on any of the beaches, and the state of Hawai'i asks that all cigarette butts be disposed of
properly. Keep in mind that alcohol is prohibited on beaches. On the following pages I have detailed the best beach locations on Maui, Kaua'i, and
Lana'i, so if you decide it's your style, then Hawai'i won't disappoint you.

beach bliss

advantages

- No location fee is charged.

- The setting is beautiful.

- Attire can be more casual.

- Modest décor and simplified planning mean less expense.

- It's perfect for "go with the flow" couples.

things to consider

- Beaches are open to the public, so expect uninvited guests.

- You may not legally rope off your ceremony, so you must select an unoccupied spot.

- With the ocean sounds and wind, hearing the ceremony can be a challenge, so be prepared.

- No confetti, rice, or bird seed may be thrown.

- If it rains, there is no backup location.

- Alcohol is prohibited.

- Many beaches have no kitchen area, no electricity, no fresh running water, no restroom facilities, and limited parking.

- Dressing rooms are unavailable, so everyone should arrive ready for the ceremony.

Makena Cove

South Maui, ten-minute drive south from Wailea

Tucked behind a lava-rock wall on the far south side of the island, Makena Cove has the feel of an undiscovered oasis, thus giving it the nickname "secret beach." The friendly company of local fishermen and their families frequent this small piece of paradise. Couples have the choice between being married with the ocean at their feet or standing on a lava-rock bluff roughly ten feet above the water. However, the name *secret beach* tends to be rather deceiving. This once best-kept secret has become popular and has made its way around the island. Arriving early allows you a better chance for privacy, but be prepared to share the beach with other couples saying "I do." If you can imagine being wed cuddled up against the Makena Coast on one of its most popular beaches, then Makena Cove is the perfect for site you.

LOCATION DETAILS: This quaint little cove can comfortably accommodate up to twenty-five seated guests. There is limited parking and no restrooms. Receptions are not recommended, but this is a perfect spot if you choose to have a dinner for two directly on the beach. The closest reputable dining options are the Prince Court at the Maui Prince Hotel and the Seawatch Restaurant in Wailea.

Makena Beach: North Maluaka Beach Park

South Maui, five-minute drive south from Wailea

If you're only looking to get your toes a little wet, North Maluaka is the perfect place to step right out of your car and onto the sand, with the ocean just a few feet away. Protected from road traffic by beach naupaka plants year-round at North Maluaka, couples can quickly exchange their vows and then enjoy a leisurely walk down the beach with a photographer trailing along to capture these once-in-a-lifetime moments. Makena Beach is one of the longest white-sand beaches on Maui, and North Maluaka is one of only two entrances to the main stretch. If this location sounds like the one for you, then it might be necessary to select a spot toward the center of the beach to avoid the entrance, which is often crowded with locals, tourists, and of course, other wedding-related activities.

LOCATION DETAILS: North Maluaka Beach offers a picturesque view of the south shore and can comfortably accommodate any number of seated guests. The beach is steps away from the entrance, and a public parking lot is a two-minute walk down the road. Public restroom facilities are available at the parking lot area and close at 7 p.m. Receptions aren't recommended, but semi-private dinners on the beach for up to six people are easily accommodated. The closest reputable dining options are the Prince Court at the Maui Prince Hotel and the Seawatch Restaurant in Wailea.

Makena Beach: South Maluaka Beach Park

South Maui, eight-minute drive south from Wailea

This beach park provides three wedding locations ranging from a very small to a somewhat large grassy area overlooking the beautiful south side of Makena Beach. Depending on the time of day and the accessibility of areas, couples can have their ceremony lit with scattered rays of sunshine breaking through the tops of keawi trees as the ocean crashes onshore. Or couples can be wed right on the beach itself, with the ocean rushing up behind them, covering their bare feet as they dig their toes into the soft wet sand. With views of the West Maui Mountains to the right and Molokini to the left, South Maluaka provides a beautiful location for an outdoor wedding. Just keep in mind that this location is a popular public beach, and with the Makena Golf Course right beside it, you should be prepared for the possibility of a few unexpected guests as well as other weddings nearby, which will simply make the occasion all the more memorable.

LOCATION DETAILS: The great thing about this location is that it offers grassy areas with picnic tables overlooking the beach. These areas, although small, can comfortably accommodate up to fifty seated guests, and the beach can accommodate any reasonable number. Two parking lots are within a two-minute walk to the beach, and restrooms are available until 7 p.m. The closest preferred dining option is the Prince Court at the Maui Prince Resort, walking distance away. Other options within a ten-minute drive include the Seawatch Restaurant, Nick's Fishmarket at the Fairmont Kea Lani, and Spago at the Four Seasons Resort.

Po'olenalena Beach

South Maui, three-minute drive south from Wailea

Being one of the most recently developed wedding locations, Po'olenalena Beach does not yet generate as much foot traffic as other beaches. With native keawi trees as a backdrop, the rugged lava-rock coastline carves itself in and out of the beach, making little coves, most of which are accessible only by water. There are three entrances to this beach that you can easily miss if you're not looking carefully. All of the entrances have gates that are regulated by the county of Maui or the Makena Surf Condos and are closed about twenty minutes after the sun sets. I have had several couples pronounce their vows on a late afternoon with no one and nothing in sight but the brilliant blue sky above and the slow-setting sun on the horizon. Even though it's a relatively new beach site, there is still a chance that you will be sharing it with other couples. And yet, if the odds are in your favor, this location will provide you with the feeling of being married on your very own tropical island.

LOCATION DETAILS: This beach can comfortably accommodate up to fifty seated guests. Access is tricky, depending on which entrance you choose. It's best to scout this location prior to your wedding day, so you can give detailed directions to your family and friends. Parking is a two-minute walk to the beach on a paved pathway. Receptions are not an option due to the access gates closing early. Keep in mind that modest (Porta Potti) restroom facilities are available at only one of the three entrances. The closest preferred dining option is the Seawatch Restaurant. Other options within a ten-minute drive include the Prince Court at Maui Prince Resort, Nick's Fishmarket at the Fairmont Kea Lani, and Spago at the Four Seasons Resort.

Kapalua Bay Beach

West Maui, fifteen-minute drive north from Ka'anapali

Once only reachable by a trek through the bushes with nothing but coconut trees as your company, Kapalua Bay Beach is now one of the most popular beaches in the Kapalua area. Flanked on one side by the Kapalua Bay Hotel and on the other by the Napili Kai Beach Club, with private condos in between, this beach is known for its majestically beautiful view of the island of Lana'i. The soft white sand tends to be quite enticing, but obvious obstacles make this site one of the livelier locations on which to hold a wedding ceremony. Because it sits on the northwest side of the island, Kapalua Bay Beach can be a bit windy or rainy during the winter months. But if you want to wed on the most scenic westside beach, where weddings, beachgoers, and watersports enthusiasts are ever present, then Kapalua Bay Beach is the beach for you.

LOCATION DETAILS: One of the most popular snorkeling spots in Hawai'i, this beautiful bay can comfortably accommodate up to seventy-five guests. The parking lot is about a one-minute walk to the beach, and group transportation is recommended as parking is very limited. Restrooms are available. Receptions are not recommended as there is limited beach access. However, semiprivate dinners on the beach can be arranged for up to six people. The closest reputable dining options are the Banyan Tree in the Ritz-Carlton, and the Plantation House Restaurant in Kapalua.

Ironwood Beach

West Maui, fifteen-minute drive north from Ka'anapali

If you've settled on the Kapalua area as your wedding destination and other sites don't quite make the cut, Ironwood Beach may be what you're looking for. Tucked away on the northern portion of west Maui, this beach is surrounded by several private residences, and most people don't even realize there is a beach here, making this a fairly private location. A popular surf spot for locals and tourists alike, with the ocean breaking just offshore and the brilliant gleam of the sun as it hits the clear, cool open water, Ironwood provides a wonderful backdrop for a wedding. If you don't mind the occasional disturbance of locals taking their dogs for a run and playing in the surf, and the small hike required to get down to the beach, then Ironwood just might be the perfect romantic location for you.

LOCATION DETAILS: Be prepared for a steep two-minute walk over somewhat rugged terrain to get down to this beach. Any number of guests willing to make the journey are welcome. However, parking is limited to eight stalls. Chairs may cost more to rent due to the lengthy hauling involved. Receptions are not recommended because of the challenging access and lack of restroom facilities. The closest reputable dining options are the Banyan Tree in the Ritz-Carlton, and the Plantation House Restaurant in Kapalua.

Hanalei Bay

Hanalei, Kaua'i, one-hour drive north from Lihu'e Airport

A short stroll from Princeville Resort is a slice of heaven called Hanalei Bay. Surrounded by mountains and cliffs that seem to carry the echoes of ancient Hawai'i, it is one of the most stunning beaches in the Hawaiian Islands. An excellent surfing spot that attracts surfers from around the world, Hanalei Bay is the largest bay on Kaua'i. A nearly perfect semicircle of white sand set against a backdrop of waterfalls and the emerald mountain peaks of the Na Molokama Mountains. Wrapped in the mist of fresh rainwater throughout most of the year, Hanalei Bay is also blessed by the ever-present beauty of the Hanalei River to the east. Falling on the west side of the bay is the Waipa River, thus allowing for every ocean and river activity imaginable.

LOCATION DETAILS: Easily accessible by car, this magnificent bay has adequate parking and can accommodate as many guests you wish. Receptions are not desirable due to unpredictable weather patterns. There is a pavilion area with picnic tables, benches, and public restroom facilities. The Princeville Resort offers the most upscale dining. You may also choose to take a ten-minute drive up the coast in either direction to the town of Kilauea or Hanalei for further options.

Ke'e Beach

Hanalei, Kaua'i, ninety-minute drive north from Lihu'e Airport

Ke'e Beach offers an inviting lagoon that is almost completely closed off by a coral reef, which makes it a nearly perfect spot to snorkel. With the reef mostly exposed at low tide, you can observe the natural marine life of the beach without even getting your nose wet. The lagoon area is so calm during the summer months that it almost seems like your very own saltwater pool. The location showcases gorgeous views of the Na Pali coastline. The trees bordering the beach provide a welcome relief from the strong tropical sun, and you can exchange your vows cooled by a slight ocean breeze. The beach tends to be crowded at certain times of the day and certain times of the year, but if you get there early in the morning, then you and your fiancé might have it all to yourselves, your own private oasis smack dab in the middle of paradise.

LOCATION DETAILS: The north shore at the foot of the Na Pali Coast, the crystal clear blue water and swaying palm trees in the distance compose a stunning backdrop for an intimate sunset wedding. The beach is at the end of the road, and there are restrooms and adequate parking. This well-kept area has picnic tables and drinking water and an ideal climate most of the year. Closest dining options are in the town of Hanalei—a twenty-minute drive away. My top two recommendations are Bamboo Bamboo Restaurant, which offers seafood and pasta, and Sushi Blues, which offers Pacific Rim dining and can accommodate larger parties.

Keoneloa Bay (Shipwreck Beach)

Po'ipu, Kaua'i, forty-minute drive south from Lihu'e Airport

Also known as Shipwreck Beach, Keoneloa Bay was named after an old wooden shipwreck that has long since disappeared, but there's still a famous ship-shaped rock on the north end. The sandy, rock-studded beach was once one of the best-hidden secrets of Kaua'i, but it's now bordered by a major resort, which makes the beach a little harder to have all to yourself. Partially protected from the strong ocean currents and high surf by cliffsides that fall into the water, swimming should still be left to only the most skilled. But seasoned surfers, boogie boarders, body surfers, and windsurfers greatly enjoy the challenge that this beach presents. You can often see the rare Hawai'ian monk seals make their way onto the beach to bask in the warm rays of the sun. Shipwreck Beach is also a great beach anytime of the year to stroll along in search of the perfect shell.

LOCATION DETAILS: Shipwreck Beach is an ideal spot for weddings, and any number of guests can join you. Public parking is available, but access is easier if you choose valet parking at the Grand Hyatt Kauai. Restrooms are available nearby. The Hyatt offers the most upscale dining. The Beach House Restaurant, Plantation Gardens, and Roy's Poipu Bar & Grill are other recommended options.

Mahaulepu Beach

Po'ipu, Kaua'i, forty-five minutes south from Lihu'e Airport

Getting to Mahaulepu Beach, one of the more popular beach parks, requires somewhat of an adventure. If you're driving, you must continue beyond the eastern end of Po'ipu Road, where the pavement gives way to a dirt road. The beach is located on private property, so be prepared to present ID and to sign a liability release at the security shack at the gate entrance. Despite this minor inconvenience, this beach can accommodate many visitors while still being an isolated and pristine location. After a short stroll, your wedding party will easily find a stretch of golden sand or a dramatic sea cliff all to yourselves. The sandy beach, carved into a rocky point, will astonish you with its wild beauty, crashing surf, and churning turquoise waters that glow with the sunlight. The spectacular views of the coastline, incredible rock formations, and sea pools that shelter tiny sea life make Mahaulepu Beach the best beach on the south shore.

LOCATION DETAILS: Gate hours are from 7:30 a.m. to 7 p.m. because you have to pass through private property to get there. Pathways from the parking area make it easy to walk directly onto the beach, but there are no restrooms. From the Grand Hyatt Kauai Resort in Koloa, it is a three-mile drive down a dirt road (allow twenty minutes because of the poor road conditions). This location offers the best chances for a private beach wedding closest to the airport. The Hyatt offers the most upscale dining. Plantation Gardens, Roy's Poipu Bar & Grill, and the Beach House Restaurant are other recommended dining options.

Kalihiwai Bay

North Shore Kaua'i, forty-five-minute drive north from Lihu'e Airport

Just outside Kilauea at the gateway to the north shore of Kaua'i is a turquoise gem of the Pacific. Surrounded by emerald green cliffs and rimmed by shady ironwood trees, the shimmering waters of Kalihiwai Bay are joined by the Kalihiwai River, which flows from the interior of the valley and provides couples with a selection of spots for a gorgeous wedding site and even lovelier photo opportunities. You'll catch your first glimpse of Kalihiwai Bay as you drive down a narrow road carved into the side of the cliff. From here you see the bay's perfect crescent-shaped white sands nestled between Ka Lae o Kowali cliffs on the west and the towering sea cliffs of Kapuka'amoi Point to the east. With the most awesome beaches in the spectacular rural area of Haena, and with gorgeous sunsets all year round, Kalihiwai Bay provides couples with an ideal setting for a truly tropical beach wedding.

LOCATION DETAILS: This beach is a favorite among the locals, but few people other than local residents frequent it. A few steps from parking will take you right to the beach, but there are no restrooms. Make sure you take the first entrance on the Kalihiwai Road before the stone bridge to get the easiest access and best parking, and to avoid crossing a small river. Princeville Resort is a ten-minute drive away and offers the most upscale dining. You may also choose to drive up the coast to either Kilauea or Hanalei for other dining options.

Hulopoʻe Beach

Lanaʻi, two-minute drive from harbor,
thirty-minute drive southwest from Lihuʻe Airport

Hulopoʻe Beach is nearly seven miles from the center of Lanaʻi City, at the end of Manele Road. It is the most popular picnicking and swimming beach on the island. A part of the Marine Life Sanctuary and underwater Marine Park, this protected beach is the safest place on the island to swim. Its beautiful white sand and underwater coral formations make it the center of recreational activity. Overlooking this idyllic spot, the Manele Bay Hotel sits on the bluff just a five-minute walk away. And, although Hulopoʻe Beach is one of the most popular destinations on Lanaʻi, it still manages to retain its immaculate appearance as if completely untouched by anyone or anything on earth.

LOCATION DETAILS: There are only a few ways anyone can get to the island of Lanaʻi. The first is hopping on Expeditions, the local ferry from Maui. The second is to book a private charter on a boat, and the third is to fly in on private or commercial aircraft. Make sure you secure ground transportation once you arrive. It's best to secure your stay at one of the resorts and arrive a day or two in advance of the wedding. The beach areas can comfortably accommodate any number of guests, and there are adequate parking and restroom facilities. Receptions are not recommended directly on the beach. The nearby Manele Bay Hotel has two wonderful restaurants, Ihilani and Hulopoʻe Court and can accommodate groups of any size.

© A & C Photography

gardens

gardens

Serenaded by running streams and waterfalls or by the sounds of native birds, the state's gardens provide an extraordinary mixture of natural settings for your wedding day. Reflecting the untouched beauty of Hawai'i, garden ceremonies allow you the chance to have a wedding amid acres of lush tropical plants and flowers from around the world. Couples can exchange vows surrounded by a showcase of hundreds of species of plants, from the exotic protea to the vibrant hibiscus bush. Incorporating various cultures—from Hawaiian and Portuguese to Japanese, Chinese, and Filipino—the tropical foliage of Hawai'i and its unsurpassed mountain and distant ocean views offer a splendid array of photo opportunities.

I remember one garden wedding with nearly a hundred people in attendance. The couple rented an elaborate Hawaiian-style arch on which native bird-of-paradise flowers were hand-carved out of the wood frame. I had a rental company deliver and set up all the chairs, and afterwards I sprinkled thousands of fragrant plumeria blossoms down the aisleway. The garden's staff was incredibly helpful and even provided potted flowers around the entrance.

Garden locations offer an abundance of amenities that include adequate restroom facilities, electrical outputs, dressing rooms, nearby parking, and catering options. Compared to resorts, garden locations tend to be a bit more challenging when it comes to the catering. You will need to bring in an outside caterer, along with many other rental items, if you are considering a reception dinner. But if a simple yet intimate ceremony in a lush tropical setting is what you have in mind, then a garden wedding may be just what you're looking for.

garden grandeur

advantages

- It offers more privacy than a beach.

- Guests will enjoy the beautiful tropical foliage and stunning views.

- Adequate parking and restroom facilities are provided.

things to consider

- The weather will be cooler.

- Beach access is limited, so you may have to forgo beach photography or pay extra for two location shoots.

- On-site food and beverage services will be minimal.

Kula Botanical Gardens

638 Kekaulike Avenue
Kula, Maui, HI 96790
808-878-1715

Established in 1968, the Kula Botanical Gardens are set at an elevation of 3,300 feet; thousands of beautiful flowers and plants cover apporximately six acres, many native to the Hawaiian Islands. Temperatures are cooler due to the elevation: summer months range in the mid-70s, while winter months range in the mid-60s. Couples have a choice of being wed on an open lawn bathed in sunlight while enjoying the cool upcountry air, or in the privacy of one of two gazebos, with some of the oldest and most unusual rock formations on the island just below them. Accompanied by the sounds of a waterfall, couples can enjoy the panoramic views of the valley and the West Maui Mountains as they gently make their way along carefully landscaped paths shortly after exchanging their vows. Couples can have a variety of tropical pictures taken: under a covered bridge festooned with white ginger flowers and ti plants, or just next to a beautifully laid-out koi pond. Outstanding views of the island, incredible hospitality, and bountiful garden areas make this location perfect for an upcountry experience.

LOCATION DETAILS: The gardens are open 9 AM to 4 PM seven days a week, all year long, holidays included. Morning wedding reservations are recommended because of the brilliant lighting, making for rare photographic opportunities. Wedding-site choices include a small or large gazebo or a lawn area. The lawn can accommodate up to 125 seated guests, and the gazebo can accommodate up to 20 guests. The location does not provide alcohol, but allows you to bring in catering. Parking is available nearby, with overflow parking a few minutes away. Restrooms are wheelchair accessible. Beach access is thirty minutes away. For reception or dinner options, Kula Lodge is a ten-minute drive away; a private reception can also be arranged in the lawn area.

GROUNDS FEES AND DEPOSITS: $50 for wedding and $50 for reception. In addition, a fee of $5.00 per person is charged for parties under twelve in number, and $4.50 per person for parties over twelve in number. A 20 percent deposit is required in advance to hold your date. Please add an additional fee of $35 per hour if garden use is after its regular business hours.

Maui Tropical Plantation

1670 Honoapiʻilani Highway
Wailuku, Maui, HI 96793
808-244-7643 or 800-451-6805
808-270-0307 (direct line, Patty Okuda)
e-mail: pattyokuda@hotmail.com
www.mauitropicalplantation.com

Maui Tropical Plantation can provide a quaint little retreat for a wedding. Many keiki (young ones) learned how to cut their first pineapples here, while others learned their first hula. A mixed plate of old Maui surrounded by exotic flowers, the spectacular West Maui Mountains as a backdrop, and the vast Haleakala Mountains in the foreground, Maui Tropical Plantation offers a number of charming sites in which to wed. Can't tell the difference between a papaya and a mango? You can go on a narrated private tram ride through sixty acres filled with papayas, mangoes, taro, macadamia nuts, coffee, and almost any other tropical fruit or flower that you could imagine. Although it lacks beach access and sunset views, the plantation's outdoor locations—ranging from a garden gazebo to several grassy areas overlooking a radiant lagoon nearby—are magnificently landscaped with swaying palm trees and lush greenery to create the perfect atmosphere for your dream outdoor wedding.

LOCATION DETAILS: The gazebo area sits off the ground and is small if you choose to wed inside it. You can seat up to one hundred guests in front of it. Champagne and alcoholic beverages are offered on-site. Locals favor this location because of its large parking area, indoor and outdoor venues, adequate restrooms, and reasonable reception costs. This location is a fifteen-minute drive to north Kihei beaches. There is a dining room available for a private dinner or reception on-site, or you can choose an outdoor area near the gazebo. The closest nearby reputable dining options include Waterfront Restaurant located at the Ma'alaea Harbor. Other restaurants in Kihei or Lahaina are a thirty-to forty-five-minute drive away.

GROUNDS FEES AND DEPOSITS: $400 for two hours of use. A $250 deposit secures your wedding date and becomes nonrefundable within ninety days of your event. The remaining balance is due a week prior to your wedding date. Additional fees are required if you decide on having your reception there.

Ali'i Kula Lavender Garden

1100 Waipoli Road
Kula, Maui, HI 96790
808-878-3004 or 808-878-8090 (for tours)
reservations@aliikulalavender.com
www.aliikulalavender.com

Nestled along the skirt of Haleakala, Ali'i Kula Lavender Gardens offer a wedding location with beauty unlike any other seen in the upcountry areas of Maui. Their sweeping views let you see the island from head to foot, and with twenty-five thousand lavender plants on beautifully landscaped property, they are the perfect setting for a unique ceremony. Nowhere else in the world can couples say "I do" amid such a variety of lavender plants, whose history dates back more than two millennia to the peoples of Arabia, Egypt, Phoenicia, and ancient Rome. Visitors to this garden enjoy guided tours and late morning tea parties, complete with homemade lavender scones and freshly brewed lavender tea. You can also wander the property on your own and pause at one of the stone benches or seating areas sprinkled about the property to gaze at the breathtaking views. And don't forget the quaint little gift shop where an entire line of lavender items made at the farm are showcased and available for you to take home or incorporate into a fragrant lavender themed wedding.

LOCATION DETAILS: A lavender-filled meadow, the Lavender Garden Lawn wedding site is one of a kind. You can choose a backdrop of Haleakala or a view of the island itself. You can decorate a built-in wooden arch, host a band on the existing stage, or have a quaint little reception on the lanai, which can host up to fifty people. Reception areas do not have electrical outlets, so generators will need to be brought in. Alcohol can be brought in. Restrooms are available, and there is a large area for parking. A private reception can be arranged on the Lavender Garden Lawn or the Ali'i Garden Terrace. Or you may prefer the Kula Lodge, which is a fifteen-minute drive away. This location is a forty-five-minute drive to the closest north shore beach.

GROUNDS FEES: $600 for two hours of use and up to fifteen people. Each additional person is $10 each, up to seventy-five people. The third hour is $300 for up to 15 people, and an additional $10 per person up to seventy-five people (maximum). Fees do not include any items that need to be rented. Hours for the wedding site are from 1:30 p.m. to sunset.

Molokini Lookout at Seawatch Restaurant

100 Wailea Golf Club Drive
Wailea, Maui, HI 96753
808-875-8080
808-875-7462 (fax)
info@seawatchrestaurant.com
www.seawatchrestaurant.com

Palm trees and massive monkey pod trees line the roadway leading up to the Seawatch Restaurant, where you can have a shuttle waiting to take your guests up to the Molokini Lookout. This spectacular venue was created specifically with the bride in mind. Carved out of the mountain and located right above the golf course, it is extremely private. A large lawn area bordered by a pink oleander hedge distinguishes the area from the nearby terrain. Immerse yourself in breathtaking views that slope down to the ocean, where you can see the island of Kaho'olawe and Molokini in the distance, a sight that makes you feel as if you are on top of the world.

LOCATION DETAILS: The informal garden setting can accommodate up to five hundred people. There is no direct beach access, but you can arrange a short drive to a nearby beach for sunset photos after the ceremony. Molokini Lookout has no music curfew, yet prepare yourself for large catering costs if you decide to have your reception there. The Seawatch Restaurant itself has a very nice, economical outdoor private reception area called the Lower Lawn, which can accommodate up to seventy people. The food and beverage is less expensive and it has more flexibility with your music, allowing you to have a small band and dance floor. You can also have a bar set up without paying bartender's fees. The Lower Lawn has a great ocean view in one direction and golf course views in the other.

GROUNDS FEES AND DEPOSITS: The Molokini Lookout site fee is $850 and includes up to thirty chairs. A $425 deposit is required to secure your wedding date; it is fully refundable up to thirty days prior to the wedding date. The remaining balance is due at least thirty days before your wedding. If you cancel between fifteen and twenty-nine days before the date, then 50 percent is refundable. If you cancel within fourteen days, the entire deposit is nonrefundable.

Na 'Aina Kai Botanical Gardens

4101 Wailapa Road
Kilauea, Kauai, HI 96754
808-828-0575 or 808-828-0525
events@naainakai.org
www.naainakai.org

Romance is always in the air at Na 'Aina Kai Botanical Gardens, a nonprofit foundation that spans 240 acres on the north shore of Kaua'i and offers its facilities for a limited number of weddings per year. This location can accommodate up to two hundred people and offers a variety of widely different options. A living mosaic of twelve diverse and bounteous gardens features one of the largest collections of bronze sculptures in the United States. Couples can choose from the Seaside venue, which is composed of two adjacent lawn areas, one for the ceremony and one for the reception, with access to Kaluakai Beach. The Ka'ula Lagoon and Garden offers three unique manicured settings that display a Japanese treehouse, arched bridges, and a cascading waterfall. The Wild Forest provides a grassy meadow in a lush woodland setting with streams under a cool tropical canopy. Yet another option is the former home of the garden's founders, known as the Residence at Na 'Aina Kai, which provides an elegant ocean-view setting (indoor and outdoor) overlooking Rock Quarry Beach. Whether you prefer an intimate wedding near one of the largest koi-filled lagoons in Hawai'i, an elaborate beachside event, or an exchange of vows in a forest of sixty thousand hardwood trees, the beauty of Na 'Aina Kai will take your breath away.

LOCATION DETAILS: Photographic opportunities are abundant with numerous water features, benches, gazebos, and sculptures. All weddings must be planned and supervised by a reputable wedding coordinator. A guesthouse may be rented as a dressing-room facility on your wedding day. There are plenty of parking spaces and adequate restrooms. There is no on-site dining facility, so any food and beverage must be provided by an outside catering company. Public dining options are available in the towns of Princeville or Kapaa, about a fifteen-minute drive away. Guided tours are also available.

GROUNDS FEES AND DEPOSITS: Minimum bookings are for three hours of use with a maximum of twenty-five people and can be secured up to six months in advance with a fee of $900. One-day events, booking up to one year in advance, run $4,000–$4,500. Three-day events can be secured for $7,500, which allows for setup the day before and breakdown the day after. Weddings at the Na 'Aina Kai residence are $5,000 a day. Reservations are made on a first-come, first-served basis. A $250 nonrefundable deposit secures your date, with the final balance due sixty days in advance.

Moir Gardens at Kiahuna

2253 Po'ipu Road
Koloa, Kauai, HI 96756
808-741-6411 or 800-outrigger
www.pgrestaurant.com

Moir Gardens and Plantation Garden Restaurant work together and are located side by side. The restaurant takes bookings and manages weddings in the garden. Moir Gardens at Kiahuna is operated by the Outrigger Hotel.

Within the beautifully restored Kiahuna Plantation you will find the stunning Moir Gardens, once part of the oldest sugar plantation in Hawai'i. Built in the style of old plantation structures, Moir Gardens comprise thirty-five acres of exotic plants and trees. Adjacent to the famous Plantation Gardens Restaurant, the site has several koi ponds, coconut trees, kou trees, a cactus garden, bromeliads, and an extensive collection of rare orchids—all of which provide a romantic setting. Couples can enjoy the pleasant subtlety of a small garden wedding or delight in the festivities of a large wedding and reception with as many as three hundred guests. Set along sweeping sandy beaches, and showcasing the intricate details of historic manor-house architecture, this garden setting provides a wonderful location for any wedding, big or small.

LOCATION DETAILS: The garden and restaurant together have one ceremony site located carefully in front of a koi pond surrounded by an orchid garden and cactus garden. The bride can make a grand entrance along the winding pathways or down a staircase from the Plantation Gardens Restaurant. The privacy is enhanced by fragrant breezes smelling of the surrounding plumeria flowers. Only acoustical music is allowed (no amplified music). The restaurant is an authentic plantation-style house that maintains the Hawaiian ancestry in its décor and menu. The restaurant is open from 5:30 p.m., only for dinner, but private-party luncheons can be arranged. Wedding cakes can be ordered through the restaurant. There are restrooms and ample parking available. The beach is a three-minute walk down a paved pathway.

GROUNDS FEES: The site fee is $100, and you can marry on the grounds only if you have your reception at the restaurant. The south lanai can be reserved for exclusive use (up to a maximum of sixty people), as can the entire restaurant. The venue price depends on the season.

McBryde Garden

4425 Lawai Road
Koloa, Kauai, HI 96756
808-742-2623
www.ntbg.org

Six million years ago the island of Kaua'i emerged from the ocean, little more than a pile of lifeless rock separated by at least two thousand miles from any great land mass. Many of the six thousand native Hawaiian species (some which are endangered), plants, and animals from that time thrive in this garden. The National Tropical Botanical Gardens (NTBG) is a private nonprofit organization comprising three botanical gardens, one of which is the McBryde. Privately funded, the NTBG is dedicated to conservation of tropical plants that are rare or endangered. Situated between rugged cliffs that drop into the picturesque Lawai Valley floor on the north shore, this garden offers couples the chance to experience an ancient part of Hawai'i as they are surrounded by the ever-elegant heliconia, orchids, and many other plants from the tropical regions of the world.

LOCATION DETAILS: The garden's visitor center, located across from Spouting Horn in Po'ipu, is open daily from 8:30 a.m. to 5:00 p.m., with trams leaving every hour on the half hour to McBryde Garden (about a fifteen-minute ride). It helps to have comfortable walking shoes, a hat for shade, bottled water, and insect repellant to thoroughly enjoy the 252-acre area. Reservations are taken on a first-come, first-served basis. Alcohol is not allowed. There is adequate parking, and restrooms are available in the visitors' center. After your return to the visitors' center you can drive to either Spouting Horn or Po'ipu Beach Park for photos. Beach House Restaurant is the most recommended within a three-minute drive. Plantation Gardens Restaurant and Roy's Poipu Bar & Grill are a five-minute drive away.

GROUNDS FEES: $15 per person

Wailua Tropical Gardens—East Side

Also known as Smith's Tropical Paradise
174 Wailua Road
Kapaa, Kauai, HI 96746
808-821-6892
www.smithskauai.com/paradise.html

In the Wailua Marina State Park, only minutes from the main highway, sit thirty acres of magnificent botanical and cultural gardens and a fern grotto. At Wailua Tropical Gardens, you can stroll through winding pathways surrounded by tropical splendor or take a narrated tram ride that will allow you to enjoy the serene atmosphere of this exotic garden. Framed by lagoons that are abundant with fish, this location is nestled alongside the lush Wailua River and also near an ancient temple, a place once reserved for Hawaiian royalty. The garden also serves as a safe haven for several unusual species of birds as well as many varieties of tropical fruit trees. Grassy areas next to the river are surrounded by coconut trees and provide a scenic backdrop for a ceremony next to the river; or you may opt to venture up the river to the famous Fern Grotto area where you can say "I do" in a natural ampitheatre setting while the misty forest blesses you with a dewy mountain atmosphere. With the cool lagoons reflecting the beauty of your wedding, the Wailua Tropical Gardens offers an elegant mixture of heritage and history to make your wedding day one to remember.

LOCATION DETAILS: This location is open daily from 8:30 a.m. to 4:00 p.m. and is the closest garden to the Lihu'e Airport, making its atmosphere very busy. Tram tours take place at 5:30 p.m., after the garden closes. Smith's

Tropical Paradise is the company that runs the garden as well as other tours nearby. There are restrooms and plenty of parking is available. A short drive across the main highway will allow you modest beach access. There is a Hawaiian luau on the property on Mondays, Wednesdays, and Fridays beginning at 6:30 p.m. Call 808-821-6893 for more luau information.

GROUNDS FEES AND DEPOSITS: Bookings are on a first-come, first-served basis. Packages for up to ten people start at $275 and include a minister, two flower leis, and a souvenir wedding certificate. There is a $5 fee for each additional person. A 50 percent deposit is required to secure your date, with the remaining balance due at least two weeks prior to your wedding day.

Kilohana Plantation

3-2087 Kaumuali'i Highway
Lihue, Kauai, HI 96766
808-245-5608 or 808-245-9593 (Gaylord's)
www.kilohanakauai.com

Kilohana Plantation stands as a reminder of an age that has since passed, offering its guests the same Island warmth as this historic plantation did more than half a century ago. You can hover over magnificent artwork and antiques in the Tudor-style mansion and roam more than thirty acres of exotic plants and gardens. Kaua'i's first mansion, the manor house at Kilohana was the most expensive and beautiful home built on the island in 1935. In 1985 Kilohana transformed itself from a private estate to commercial property. The bedrooms, the carriage house, and the guest cottages have become upscale gift shops, offering a range of Island-made products such as clothing, jewelry, Hawaiian quilts, and more. To better enjoy the beautifully restored grounds, couples can take a carriage ride through this elegant plantation property. With the pride of Kaua'i's golden age, Kilohana Plantation offers indoor and outdoor locations on which to wed with on-site dining at its restaurant, so you can enjoy your ceremony and reception in the same location. The property lies between two towns, so that even though you're right off the highway, you are in a serene oasis with complete privacy. Tents and themed events can be arranged to create one of the most beautiful settings in all of Kaua'i.

LOCATION DETAILS: Hours are from 9:30 a.m. to 9:30 p.m. This location can accommodate more than five hundred people. You can take a twenty-minute carriage ride for $10 or an hour carriage ride on Monday, Tuesday, or Thursday for $24; both run daily from 11 a.m. to 6 p.m. The courtyard is absolutely amazing. It is home to Gaylord's, which offers exquisite dining morning, noon, and night with Hawaiian-themed luaus twice a week, which makes this location very desirable for receptions. There are restrooms and adequate parking is available. Alcohol is provided by the gardens only; corkage fees will apply if you bring your own. Other dining options off the property include the Poipu Beachhouse Restaurant, Plantation Gardens Restaurant, and Roy's Poipu Bar & Grill. Kalapaki Bay is the nearest beach, about a ten-minute drive away (it fronts the Marriott).

GROUNDS FEES: $150 fee for a natural-setting location. Décor enhancements (arches, chairs, runner, carriage, and so on) are extra. Different rooms can be opened for cocktails or dinners. Carriage house ($500) and tented events are available for larger groups. The staff can help you coordinate your event and create a package within your budget. The venue Eiliahi, a twenty-minute drive up in the mountains from the plantation, can also be reserved for $3,500. Catering off-site is welcomed, and there are a variety of sites to select from. Reserving the entire site and restaurant exclusively for your group costs $10,000, plus a minimum food and beverage charge.

© Bill Stockwell

resorts

resots

Combining a sense of history with contemporary elegance and natural beauty, the resorts of Hawai'i beckon hopeless romantics in search of a luxurious haven. With exclusive services, first-rate restaurants, and cultured entertainment, Island resorts offer an endless array of amenities with a gracious aloha spirit. Millions of dollars and countless hours have gone into providing couples with beautiful settings and photo opportunities unlike those offered anywhere else. Many resorts sit on some of the best beaches in the world, so you will be able to make use of the entire property, not only for the wedding site and beach photos but also for receptions and private romantic dinners. With caretakers constantly maintaining the grounds, resorts showcase magnificently designed water features, elaborate gardens highlighted with brilliantly colored flowers, bridges, gazebos, benches, and more.

Couples also have the option of staying at the resort, where they can get dressed and have their hair and makeup done in their rooms, all the while having a ministore and shops close at hand. If you choose to stay at a resort other than the one where you are getting married, temporary, shared courtesy rooms are often available for you to get ready in, free of charge. Otherwise, some resorts offer a half-day room rental specifically for use as a dressing room prior to the ceremony. Both of those options depend on how busy the hotel or resort is, so please check with your planner or resort contact for more information.

Reception opportunities are endless. However, indoor ballrooms and banquet rooms do not allow open flame. Most resorts offer battery-powered votive candles, and believe it or not, they look great. Outdoor events have a music curfew of 9 or 10 p.m. Younger couples often choose to have an outdoor event up until the curfew time and then invite their guests to move into a ballroom or meet at a nightclub for music and dancing later in the evening.

On any island you visit, you will be fortunate to immerse yourself in the unique experiences that only the resorts of Hawai'i can provide. Indulge in Hawai'i's distinctive style and its blend of attentive service, expressive décor, and unforgettable dining amid acres of tropical elegance.

resort romance

advantages

- Resorts offer breathtaking garden and beach venues for the ceremony and photo opportunities.

- On-site food and beverage services are provided.

- You can book your stay at the resort itself.

- Public and private dining options are abundant.

- Impeccable service and amenities, including valet parking, is a matter of course.

things to consider

- Grounds fees and nonrefundable deposits are high, and the fees are not waived even if you are staying at a resort.

- Privacy is limited.

- Some locations don't allow a booking prior to thirty days out.

- Most outdoor receptions have an early music curfew.

- Some resorts encourage you to use their preselected vendors, so your options may be limited.

- Resorts cater to various incentive groups and conventions as well as weddings, so there may be competition for the staff's time.

Maui Prince Hotel

5400 Makena Alanui Drive
Makena, Maui, HI 96753
808-874-1111 or 866-774-6236
www.princeresortshawaii.com

Located on Makena Beach, the Maui Prince Hotel prides itself on being secluded from the other resorts located in Wailea. A small cascading waterfall sits amidst a beautifully sculpted oriental garden where a stream gently flows into a brilliantly colored koi fish pond. Reminiscent of a traditional Japanese garden, serene best describes this intimate setting. This location can accommodate parties of any size with four wedding locations. In the upper courtyard the bride is shielded by ginger stalks as she approaches her wedding party, accompanied by the sounds of a running waterfall in the background. In the lower courtyard, the bride and groom has the waterfall as a backdrop, exchanging vows with a koi pond at their feet as the sun bounces off the surface of the water. Both of these courtyards are carefully placed near the center of the hotel. Couples can have their weddings blanketed by the blue sky above and the ballroom a few feet away, should they decide to use the hotel facilities for their wining and dining pleasure.

The Maui Prince Resort also offers Pacific Lawn, Maluaka Lawn, both of which sits high above the ocean and Makena Beach, only a short stroll from the hotel. These two settings are located off to the side of the main pathway providing a grassy oasis with breathtaking views. Couples may also choose these ocean view lawn areas for their reception following a more intimate inner courtyard ceremony. Whichever location you decide, the Prince offers four unique wedding location that is removed from "hotel row".

LOCATION DETAILS: Available on a first-come, first-served basis. The upper courtyard can accommodate up to one hundred seated guests, the lower courtyard can accommodate up to ten seated guests, and the two lawns overlooking the ocean can accommodate more than one hundred guests. The inner courtyards are located in the center of the hotel on the ground level and are fairly close together. Staff can block your selected area off during the ceremony yet the general public will be able to witness your event while walking on the surrounding pathways or from the balconies above. All locations tend to be a bit breezy. There is plenty of public parking, and the roomy restrooms can be used as dressing rooms.

GROUNDS FEES AND DEPOSITS: $1,500 for nonholidays and $2,000 for holidays. The hotel will tentatively hold your reservation for seven days to give you ample time to send in your nonrefundable grounds fee deposit and confirmation booking form. There is an extra $200 fee per hour if you choose to have your ceremony at one of the ocean-view settings and want to take photographs in the inner courtyard. If you are staying at the hotel and are getting married elsewhere, then the resort will charge you $500 per hour to take photos on the property. Bookings can be secured up to six months in advance for weddings, and eight months in advance for a wedding and reception. There is also a wedding reception location fee of $1,000 for nonholiday bookings; the entire fee with tax is nonrefundable and immediately due at the time of booking.

Food and beverage: In-house only
Wedding sites: Pacific Lawn, Maluaka Lawn, upper courtyard, lower courtyard
Public receptions: Prince Court, Hakone
Private receptions: Luau Garden, ballroom and lanai, Pacific Lawn, Maluaka Lawn
Beach access: Makena Beach is a two-minute walk from the inner courtyard

Fairmont Kea Lani

4100 Wailea Alanui Drive
Wailea, Maui, HI 96753
808-875-4100 or 800-257-7544
www.fairmont.com/kealani

One of the newer editions to the island of Maui, this resort is unlike any other. The hotel's all-white façade and many arches, pillars, and alcoves give it a look reminiscent of an Egyptian palace. For some couples happily ever after begins with a wedding on one of two available sites. The first includes a semiprivate area known as the Tropical Gazebo, at the base of a three-tiered terrace. With a grand fountain as the terrace's centerpiece, guests sit off to the side as the ceremony takes place. However, the gazebo area lacks an ocean view, so you may prefer the Pacific Terrace. An ideal oceanfront setting for small gatherings, this location overlooks Polo Beach with the islands of Lana'i, Molokini, and Kaho'olawe in the background. Both locations offer you the chance to celebrate the beginning of your journey together as a wedded couple in exotic settings.

LOCATION DETAILS: The Tropical Gazebo sits at the bottom of a row of water fountains called the Royal Fountain Gardens, which can comfortably seat sixty guests. It has a terrific grand entrance opportunity, because the bride can start at the top of the stairs and descend with music as she approaches the officiant. The gazebo was recently remodeled to be lighter and brighter with no foliage on or around it. It is fairly private with no guests encroaching on the area; however, there is a kids' club nearby and sometimes you can hear pool activity. The footing is cement rather than grass, so it's not as lush as other locations.

The Pacific Terrace, near the beach, can comfortably seat thirty guests. It's made of flagstone set in a semicircle. There are public pathways on both sides and below, so people are constantly passing by, and it's very warm because of its exposure to the sun. Polo Beach Lawn is your third option and caters to extremely large groups. Located between the public pathway bordering Polo Beach and the FKL's private villas, this large grassy area is filled with palm trees and a spectacular ocean view. Perfect for large weddings in which privacy is not an issue.Public parking is available, but valet parking is best. The restrooms are large enough to use as dressing rooms.

GROUNDS FEES: $3,500. No bookings are accepted prior to ninety days out unless you confirm your stay at the hotel, then it's up to one year. If you're not a guest and getting married there, it may be possible to have some of your wedding photographs taken on the property as long as there are no other weddings confirmed on your date.

Food and beverage: In-house only
Wedding sites: Royal Fountain Gazebo, Pacific Terrace, Polo Beach Lawn
Public receptions: Nick's Fishmarket
Private receptions: Polo Beach Lawn, Palm Court, lobby mezzanine
Beach access: Polo Beach is a three-minute walk from the lobby

Four Seasons Resort Maui

3900 Wailea Alanui Drive
Wailea, Maui, HI 96753
808-874-8000
www.fourseasons.com/maui/

If ever there was a promise of paradise, the Four Seasons Resort is it. With distant views of Wailea Beach, tasteful architecture, low lighting, and fine art enhancing the lobby, the Four Seasons is as close to a Hawaiian palace as you can get, and it can accommodate the most refined and sophisticated clientele. The Four Seasons offers three wedding locations: Ocean Front Lawn, Ku'uipo Point, and a cast-iron gazebo on the fifth floor. Each of the locations sits high on a bluff offering spectacular views of Wailea Beach and the West Maui Mountains. The oceanfront lawn can accommodate large parties while Ku'iupo Point and the gazebo provide a more intimate setting for smaller groups. Whichever location you select, the resort services only one wedding at a time, making you feel like you have the place all to yourselves. Have your hair and makeup done in your room, or enjoy a restful massage or rejuvenating spa treatment and relax while the wedding of your dreams is being coordinated by the on-site wedding department. Couples looking for flawless service, award-winning cuisine, and spectacular ocean views can find exactly what they're looking for at the Four Seasons Resort.

LOCATION DETAILS: This resort does only one wedding or event on any given day and can accommodate more than one hundred guests. You must purchase a wedding package in order to marry at this resort. All wedding venues sit high above the ocean offering incredible views. Discounts of 20 percent are sometimes available on certain rooms to confirmed clients. Valet parking is available at $12 per day, and restrooms can be used as dressing rooms if you are staying off-site. The Four Seasons has incredible catering services and will guarantee you an impeccable level of service for receptions on-site or off.

GROUNDS FEES AND DEPOSITS: This resort works with packages and customizes from there. The minimum package is $8,200, and its most expensive is $45,000. There is a $2,000 nonrefundable deposit to secure your day.

Food and beverage: In-house only
Wedding sites: Ku'uipo Point, Luau Garden, fifth-floor gazebo, suites with private outdoor grassy area
Public receptions: Spago, Ferraro's Bare Ristorante
Private receptions: Luau Garden, private cabana, Ku'uipo Point, Spago's private dining room, gazebo area, in-suite dining, ballroom
Beach access: The public beach is a few minute walk that descends down to Wailea Beach

Grand Wailea Resort

3850 Wailea Alanui Drive
Wailea, Maui, HI 96753
808-875-1234 or 800-888-6100
www.grandwailea.com

One of the largest and most luxurious resorts on Maui, the Grand Wailea Resort accommodates lifestyles ranging from the modest to the most elaborate. Its grand waterfall entrance and elaborate sculptures lining the marble hallways have greeted some of the Islands' most famous visitors. Simply watch as the day you've dreamed of unfolds. Whether you select the romantic and intimate chapel, an oceanfront lawn, or a picturesque gazebo for your ceremony, the Grand Wailea will make your wedding day a day to remember. The Wailea Seaside Chapel, with its elegant surroundings, allows for the most intimate of wedding ceremonies. Surrounding the stylish chapel are seven formal gardens overflowing with gorgeous flowers, koi fish ponds, cascading waterfalls, and wedding gazebos. Here you will find some of the most peaceful settings in which to say "Aloha wai ea oi e ku'uipo" (I love you, my sweetheart) in the true spirit of aloha, all with the services of this lovely resort.

LOCATION DETAILS: This resort is very large, offering you an endless number of photo opportunities. There is an amazing waterfall at the front entrance. The Seaside Chapel is uniquely Hawaiian and offers the utmost privacy. The pews can seat 50, and you can add rental chairs to accommodate up to 125 guests. If your wedding falls on a Friday, Saturday, or Sunday, the chapel can be reserved up to six months in advance. If your wedding falls on any other day of the week, it can be reserved one year in advance. The gazebo wedding locations are near public pathways and can accommodate up to 20 standing guests. I recommend the gazebos for photos or having a small cake and champagne reception after your chapel wedding. Other locations include extremely large lawn areas that can only be reserved within ninety days of the ceremony. Valet parking is required. The restrooms can be used as dressing rooms if you are staying off-site.

GROUNDS FEES AND DEPOSITS: $3,700 (sunset), $3,200 (daytime) for a 1.5-hour time slot, of which 50 percent is nonrefundable and has to be paid at the time of booking. The remaining balance is due thirty days prior to the wedding date. If you cancel within two weeks, you will be charged full price. Grounds fees go up 6 percent annually.

Food and beverage: In-house only
Wedding sites: Seaside Chapel, gazebo garden, chapel lawn, oceanfront lawns, and overlooks
Public receptions: Humuhumunukunukuapua'a, Bistro Molokini, Kincha
Private receptions: Grand dining room, two overlook locations, oceanfront lawns, ballrooms
Beach access: Wailea Beach is a four minute walk from the lobby

Diamond Hawaii Resort

555 Kaukahi Street
Wailea, Maui, HI 96753
808-874-0500 or 800-800-0720
www.diamondresort.com

Nestled in the slopes of south Maui, Diamond Hawaii Resort is an untapped destination. Perched 300 feet above the beautiful Wailea coastline, with its uniquely Japanese-themed accommodations, this resort is just off the beaten path. On a clear day, Diamond Hawaii offers stunning views of Kaho'olawe, Lana'i, and Molokini while at the same time being just far enough away from the daily hustle and bustle of Wailea to give guests a sense of ultimate privacy. Once a retreat for affluent Japanese visitors, today Diamond Hawaii specializes in presenting an authentic Japanese experience for all guests, from fine dining to traditional Japanese spa baths, to richly landscaped gardens. It is suitable for any wedding, small or large, formal or casual. With a romantic gazebo positioned within a grassy overlook, Diamond Hawaii provides couples with silence, peace, solitude, and gorgeous views. The resort also offers poolside dining with floating candles, making your reception one of a kind.

LOCATION DETAILS: The beautiful gazebo is used mostly as a backdrop for the wedding. Unlike most other gazebos, it does not have a public pathway running next to it. This location is more remote than your typical beachfront resort. Photos can be taken on the beach, a two-minute drive away. One drawback is that the driveway entrance runs about two hundred feet in front of the gazebo, and it is not blocked off with any foliage. You may see and or hear vehicles during your ceremony, but the resort is generally quiet, given its location. Parking is available. Restrooms can be used as dressing rooms.

GROUNDS FEES AND DEPOSITS: $1,000 (includes up to twenty chairs). Additional chairs are $2.50 each. At the time of booking, 50 percent of the nonrefundable grounds fee is required and remaining charges are due one month prior to the wedding day. A water station is available upon request at no charge. However, there are setup/attendant fees if you want to have cake and/or champagne at the location, based on head count (about $2.50 each). The refund for cancellation is 100 percent if it's before thirty days of the event. Please be prepared to pay a cleanup fee to gather and clear away any personal items, decorations, rose petals, or other items.

Food and beverage: In-house only
Wedding sites: Gazebo lawn
Public receptions: Le Gunji, Restaurant Taiko, Capische
Private receptions: Pool deck, gazebo lawn
Beach access: None. The closest beach is Polo Beach, in front of the Fairmont Kea Lani, approximately a two-minute drive away

Hyatt Regency Maui Resort

200 Nohea Kai Drive
Lahaina, Maui, HI 96761
808-667-4430 or 808-661-1234
www.maui.hyatt.com

Specializing in creative Maui weddings, this Hyatt resort offers four stylish wedding sites right in the heart of Ka'anapali. The Oriental Gardens overlook a shimmering lagoon, with cascading waterfalls in the background. The area is surrounded by a public pathway on one side and the Swan Court Lagoon on the other, which provides an oasis for koi fish, flamingos, and swans. Slightly more protected from the public on the upper lobby level, the Statue Gardens are highlighted by ornamental bougainvillea vines and enhanced by the sweet smell of plumeria flowers. Ceremonies take place on a grassy bluff accentuated by an exotic array of Asian sculptures and breathtaking views of the Pacific Ocean. Ideal for the perfect Island-style wedding ceremonies, this garden can not only provide a romantic candlelit dinner for two under the stars, but can also house receptions. The staff at the Hyatt will not stop until your flowers, dinner reservations, and honeymoon are all set, making ordering breakfast in bed your biggest concern.

LOCATION DETAILS: The Statue Gardens make up a semiprivate grassy area on the lobby level of the resort. Bordering it is a four-foot-high wall with a colorful bougainvillea hedge nestled behind it. This location can comfortably seat up to eighty people. A nearby lounge has live music and begins serving right at sunset, so having your ceremony take place before the lounge opens is a must. The

Oriental Gardens are in a public area on the beach level. The actual wedding area is a small slate-rock circle that can comfortably seat twenty people. There is a wide waterfall and lagoon that serve as your backdrop with ocean views off to the side. The pathway leading to this site can be blocked off during the ceremony so that the public doesn't directly encroach on the area. The Hyatt's nightly luau begins at 5:30, and the music can be heard in the distance. The chapel is right in the middle of the Hyatt's shopping district, and the gazebo is in the middle of a public pathway, so neither of those are preferred wedding sites. Plenty of parking is available.

GROUNDS FEES AND DEPOSITS: $3,500, plus a mandatory $60 attendant's fee will be charged if you have chairs, cake, or champagne. A $500 refundable security deposit is due at the time of booking and will be returned after the wedding, or you can use it toward food and beverage. The $500 also covers damages that may occur on the property during your event. White folding chairs are available at no charge. Sites can be reserved anytime in advance.

Food and beverage: In-house only
Wedding sites: Statue Gardens, Oriental Gardens, wedding gazebo, Napili Lawn, Lokahi Chapel
Public receptions: Sonz Restaurant, Weeping Banyan, Cascades Grille, Spat's Trattoria
Private receptions: Oceanfront lawn, Statue Gardens, pool deck, ballroom
Beach access: Ka'anapali Beach is steps away

Westin Maui

2365 Ka'anapali Parkway
Kaanapali, Maui, HI 96761
808-667-2525
www.westinmaui.com

Have every detail of your wedding tailored to your specific needs by the Westin Maui. Offering two main wedding locations, the Westin can accommodate many guests for wedding ceremonies and receptions. A long walk from the main lobby area with various staircased pathways on the way, the first location is the Hale Aloha Gazebo on the upper courtyard level. This gazebo is the perfect setting for an intimate ceremony surrounded by soft flowing streams, beautiful exotic flowers, and gorgeous ocean views. The second location is a waterfall area known as the Aloha Pavilion. One of the more expensive venues, this location is set on the lower level at the back of the hotel amid cascading waterfalls and swaying palm trees—perfect for a moonlit reception under the stars with friends and family.

LOCATION DETAILS: This busy resort is in the heart of Ka'anapali, so you cannot expect privacy during picture taking. There is a huge waterfall near the entrance where you can take pictures (even while you're underneath it). This resort often hosts more than one wedding at a time, so be prepared to run into another party. The gazebo, which holds up to twenty people, is somewhat private with a distant ocean view, yet its position along the pathway is unique. The Aloha Pavilion, which holds up to sixty people, is a fairly private large open area that does not offer a direct ocean view. The waterfall backdrop is beautiful but also makes the ceremony difficult to hear, so you will have to rent audio equipment for your guests. The pavilion area is large enough to host your wedding reception right after the ceremony or even serve as a backup location in case of inclement weather. Parking is available, and although rest-rooms can be used as a dressing room, I suggest reserving a guest room for this purpose.

GROUNDS FEES: The gazebo runs $1,800. You may book the gazebo anytime in advance. The Aloha Pavilion costs $7,500. The pavilion cannot be secured on a definite basis prior to three months in advance of your wedding date. Both locations require a nonrefundable deposit.

Food and beverage: In-house only
Wedding locations: Gazebo, Aloha Pavilion
Public receptions: Tropica, Ono Bar & Grille
Private receptions: Private cabana, Aloha Pavilion
Beach access: Ka'anapali Beach is steps away

Ritz-Carlton Kapalua

1 Ritz-Carlton Drive
Kapalua, Maui, HI 96761
808-669-6200 or 800-262-8440
www.ritzcarlton.com/resorts/kapalua

A Ritz-Carlton wedding seems to set the standard for romantic elegance. Offering some of the best and most comprehensive services, the Ritz-Carlton Kapalua can create the most elaborate ceremonies—or the most simple. You can choose a ceremony in the recently renovated chapel or one performed on a lava point with the surf pulsing below. The ocean views are incredible anywhere on this property, so photo opportunities are abundant. The small and quaint Honolua Chapel is laced in Hawaiian heritage. The gazebo area positioned to the left of the chapel entrance offers a lovely area for a traditional outdoor wedding. The expansive Beach House Lawn is ideal for larger wedding and reception parties, and couples can then enjoy a traditional Hawaiian luau. The Napili Lawn—a cliffside area near the picturesque Kapalua Bay Golf Course—is set against a tremendous backdrop; watch the blazing Hawaiian sun as it sets behind the island of Lana'i with the raging surf below.

LOCATION DETAILS: The Ritz-Carlton property is extremely large and spread out. Being on the far west side of the island, it also tends to experience much more wind and rain than other locations, making it a very tropical venue. The Beach House Lawn, which is near the ocean, can accommodate groups of one hundred or more. The Napili Lawn is somewhat remote and suitable for groups of thirty or fewer. Custom transportation to and from each location is highly recommended. The beach is a ten-minute walk from the lobby of the hotel or a five-minute drive away. Plenty of parking is available.

GROUNDS FEES AND DEPOSITS: The Honolua Chapel and gazebo together are $2,700. The Napili Lawn, Beach House Lawn, and Lava Point are $2,200 each. Fifty percent of the grounds fee is required as a nonrefundable deposit, with the remaining balance due thirty days prior to your event.

Food and beverage: In-house only
Wedding sites: Lava Point, Beach House Lawn, Honolua Chapel and gazebo
Public receptions: Banyan Tree and The Terrace at the Ritz-Carlton
Private receptions: Anuenue Room, Beach House Lawn, Plantation Ballroom
Beach access: Ten-minute walk from the lobby of the hotel

Hotel Hana Maui

P.O. Box 9
Hana, Maui, HI 96713
808-248-8211 or 800-321-4262
www.hotelhanamaui.com

Celebrate your marriage with a heavenly beginning at Hotel Hana Maui. One of the most romantic resorts in the world, this location offers a range of wedding services. Tucked away in the remote part of Maui at the end of the Hana Highway, this resort offers complete relaxation and seclusion in the midst of unmatched beauty. You can reach Hana town by driving approximately three hours from central Maui, enjoying scenic overlooks, waterfalls, rain forests, and tropical splendors along the way. The road itself is an adventure with nearly 600 curves and 52 one-lane bridges. If the journey seems a bit much, you can opt to rent a private plane or helicopter to charter you in. For fifty years this casual but luxurious vacation destination has been a favorite for weddings, honeymoons, and romantic getaways. Within the most tropical area of Maui, this location, however beautiful, also receives more rain than other parts of the island. With dramatic ocean and mountain views, couples can choose from a variety of grassy areas; and from cake selection to the design of the perfect bridal bouquet, the hotel staff will help you to create the wedding of your dreams.

LOCATION DETAILS: This high-end Hawaiian-themed venue is an extremely large property. You can choose from the garden pool, Kai Halulu overlook, or the Wananalua Congregational Church nearby. This hotel also manages a plantation guesthouse, a private Hawaiian-style home with sweeping views of the ocean that can be used as a rare wedding or reception location. Located on the far east side of the island, it is in the heart of the jungle, so you should be prepared for the possibility of inclement weather. Parking is available, but the restrooms are not ideal for dressing rooms.

GROUNDS FEES: Garden pool and Kai Halulu overlook are $1,000. The plantation guesthouse is $2,500. Wedding packages start at $1,600 and include the minister, lei exchange or bouquet and boutonniere, and transportation to and from the wedding site.

Food and beverage: In-house only
Wedding sites: Variety of outdoor grassy locations, garden pool, Kai Holulu overlook, Wananalua Congregational Church, plantation guesthouse
Public receptions: Main dining room, Hana Ranch Restaurant (Wednesday, Friday, and Saturday nights)
Private receptions: Garden pavilion, Hamoa Beach and pavilion, plantation guesthouse
Beach access: Complimentary shuttle service is provided to Hamoa Beach, a five- to ten-minute drive away

Grand Hyatt Kauai

1571 Po'ipu Road
Koloa, Kauai, HI 96756
808-742-1234
www.kauai.hyatt.com

With fifty acres of meticulously manicured tropical gardens, sun-splashed pools, and open-air courtyards, the Hyatt offers a backdrop of natural splendor. Overlooking Shipwreck Beach, this popular resort is only twenty minutes from Lihu'e Airport. Its vibrantly green surroundings, spread beneath rolling mountains, provide couples with a number of pristine lawn areas on which to wed. The Regency Club Lawn plays host to the largest of groups and even has an ocean view. There is a traditional gazebo built into the far end of the lawn giving couples the option of saying "I do" in the perfect garden-style setting. Following the wedding, you can have a reception in one of five restaurants on the property, or in an outdoor area that offers private catering services. Whatever your preference, you can experience the Hawai'i you've always imagined, with sparkling waters, aromatic flowers, and beaches of ivory all at your disposal.

LOCATION DETAILS: This property is done on a grand scale and it will take you several minutes to walk down to the wedding location and beach from your room. The Hyatt offers a huge grassy lawn area surrounded by a garden. You can choose to use their existing built in gazebo for a backdrop or simply create your own. Once at the wedding location, you'll find the beach only a few feet away. DJs are allowed if you choose to have your reception on the lawn afterwards. Parking and restrooms are available.

GROUNDS FEES AND DEPOSITS: $1,800 with a $500 nonrefundable deposit to secure your wedding date. The balance is due prior to your wedding day.

Food and beverage: In-house only
Wedding location site: Gazebo, Regency Club Lawn
Public receptions: Tidepools, Dondero's
Private receptions: Private beachside setting, outdoor lawns, ballrooms
Beach access: Shipwreck Beach is a five-minute walk from the lobby

Princeville Resort

5520 Ka Haku Road
Princeville, Kauai, HI 96722
808-826-9644 or 800-826-4400
www.princeville.com/weddings

Let your pleasantly sun-drenched days turn into soft candlelit nights as the fragrance of exotic flowers mixes with pure romance at the Princeville Resort. The most elaborate resort on the island of Kaua'i, with plantation-style wood furniture, original oil prints, and Juliet balconies, the Princeville sits gracefully on Pu'u Poa Ridge, terraced along the bluff facing Hanalei Bay. Indulge in luxury at the legendary Makana Terrace or Bay Terrace restaurant on the eighth floor, with the waterfall-laced mountains of Na Molokama in the background, or choose to marry under a natural-tree archway at the rare and unique Kamani Cove. As valleys carve their way through hills of antique green to the deep blue ocean that seems to stretch to infinity, the Princeville Resort opens a gateway of an astonishing array of wedding and reception venues with the attentive, friendly service that can only be found in Hawai'i.

LOCATION DETAILS: The Makana Terrace has a complete ocean view. The Bay Terrace has a spectacular Bali Hai view. Both are nestled on the eighth floor, which itself opens to some of the most breathtaking views anywhere. Tasteful railings with pots of bougainvillea enhance each of these locations. You can access the beach in two ways: You can take a five-minute walk down a public stairway off the lobby; or you can take two elevators to land you on the beach floor. Kamani Cove is the most popular wedding site: It's on the side of the beach bordering a lava-rock edge, allowing both a sandy and a grassy environment. This location was named after the kamani trees that have formed a natural and native-style archway. There are restrooms and plenty of public parking.

GROUNDS FEES AND DEPOSITS: $2,000 for the site, which can be booked within six months before the event without a room contract. Packages start at $2,450 and include an abundance of services. A $1,000 nonrefundable deposit secures your wedding date, with the balance due fourteen days prior to your event.

Food and beverage: In-house only
Wedding locations: Makana Terrace, Bay Terrace, beach and Hanalei Bay, Kamani Cove
Public receptions: Café Hanalei, La Cascata Mediterranean Restaurant, luau dinner show on Mondays and Thursdays
Private receptions: Private cabana dinner, poolside tent, Makana Room, Bay Terrace (minimum $750 site fee for Bay Terrace)
Beach access: Hanalei Beach is a five-minute drive away

Kauai Marriott Resort & Beach Club

3610 Rice Street
Lihue, Kauai, HI 96766
808-245-5050 or 800-220-2925
www.marriott.com/property/propertypage/lihhi

Located just ten minutes from Lihu'e Airport on Kalapaki Beach, this resort drops down a lush hillside to a crescent beach, giving couples a chance to awaken their souls on one of the most amazing islands in the Hawaiian chain. The Kaua'i Marriott makes it easy to be swept into the spirit of paradise with its wide white-sand beach and carefully maintained gardens as the fragrance of tropical blossoms fill the air. The incredibly large ocean setting site at the Luau Grounds overlooking Kalapaki Beach is amazing. This lawn can accommodate hundreds and is limited only by your imagination. Section an area off with six foot palm trees, bring in a gazebo, Hawaiian kahilis, or tropical topiaries sitting on top of bamboo poles to create a dream altar area. Adding chairs and a carpet of flora for the bride to float down the isle way creates an intimate setting no matter what size ceremony you have. The Kaua'i Marriott combines warm Island hospitality with impeccable service to create a truly unforgettable wedding.

LOCATION DETAILS: The expansive garden wedding site is set in the main courtyard of the hotel. The walkway around it extends into a grassy area within the garden, and an overhang of the hotel helps to shelter you from the sunlight. There is also a small waterfall. The ocean setting at the Luau Garden is on a small cliff area with the beautiful Nawiliwili Harbor and mountain range as your backdrop. This location is huge, making it completely exposed to the elements as well as passersby. Both locations include white plastic lawn chairs for your guests. There are restrooms and plenty of parking is available.

GROUNDS FEES AND DEPOSITS: There is a $250 rehearsal site fee when applicable. The grounds fee for a 10:00 a.m., 1:00 p.m., or 4:30 p.m. ceremony is $1,900. A nonrefundable deposit of $500 is required to secure your date. Full payment is due thirty days prior to your event. Some holidays are subject to an additional $500 fee.

Food and beverage: In-house only
Wedding locations: Garden or ocean-view setting
Public receptions: Terrace Restaurant at Kaua'i Lagoons, Kukui's, Aupaka Terrace, and Duke's
Private receptions: Ballroom, specific areas on the property
Beach access: Nawiliwili Beach Park is a five-minute drive away

Sheraton Kauai Resort

2440 Hoonani Road
Koloa, Kauai, HI 96756
808-742-1661 or 866-716-8109
www.sheraton-kauai.com

In a place where falling coconuts are your biggest distraction, where clocks are rarely consulted, and *traffic* is just a word in the dictionary, relaxation awaits you at the Sheraton Kauai Resort. Once a playground for Hawaiian chiefs, the Sheraton Kauai now plays host to families and fun-seeking couples who've come to enjoy unlimited activities, subtle luxuries, and breathtaking natural surroundings. The picturesque Pacific and golden shoreline of Po'ipu Beach, coupled with warm sunny days and cool evenings, make this a perfect place to relax and get married. Available for larger ceremonies is the Garden Wing Lawn within the hotel grounds. The Point wedding site is a grassy setting overlooking Po'ipu Beach. It is directly on the water's edge, so you can have your wedding on a grassy area and then step onto the beach for photographs. Both options offer a place where life seems effortless. Spread out over twenty acres of prime oceanfront property, the Sheraton Kauai also offers a number of reception options, from fine dining in one of four elegant restaurants to private outdoor dinners for just the two of you, beckoning couples for moonlit strolls and stolen kisses under a blanket of stars.

LOCATION DETAILS: The Garden Wing Lawn is somewhat protected from the gentle breezes that constantly embrace the property. It's a long grassy area in the center of a U-shaped wing, making the area feel warm and intimate. This location can comfortably seat seventy-five people. The downside is that there is no ocean view. The Point, which does have an ocean view, is cozy, suitable for twenty guests or fewer. The Point is not available between 5 and 6 p.m. The Point restaurant has a nice atmosphere and is located right next to The Point, making it a convenient to have your reception there. Plenty of parking and restrooms are available.

GROUNDS FEES AND DEPOSITS: If you are staying at the resort, the grounds fee is $700, and a $250 nonrefundable deposit is due to secure your wedding date. The balance is due within thirty days of your event. Additional fees may be incurred if your wedding start time is after 4:30 p.m. If you are not staying at the resort and would like to use the property for your wedding, then there is an additional $500 service fee.

Food and beverage: In-house only
Wedding sites: Garden Wing Lawn (no ocean view) or The Point
Public receptions: Shells Steak & Seafood, Naniwa, The Point (on the property); Beach House Restaurant, Plantation Gardens, Roy's Poipu Bar & Grill
Private receptions: Poipu Ballroom, ballroom foyer, Koloa Room, Lawai Room, custom requests for outdoor areas
Beach access: Po'ipu Beach is steps away

Kauai Beach Hotel and Resort

4331 Kauai Beach Drive
Lihue, Kauai, HI 96766
808-245-1955 or 888-805-3843
www.kauaibeachhotelandresort.com

With cascading waterfalls and dramatic rockscape pools, Kauai Beach Hotel and Resort is a paradise unto itself. Sitting on twenty-five lavishly landscaped acres, this oceanfront resort offers the warm hospitality and top-notch service sure to please even the most particular of couples. It is also ideal for large ceremonies able to accommodate up to 450 people. On site wedding locations have a laid back and relaxed atmosphere. Choose from their oceanfront lawn, their garden grotto area, or simply choose to bury your feet in the sand on the beach fronting the resort. An arch is available and included with some of their packages. The two on-site restaurants feature aged steaks and fresh local seafood served in a Polynesian-style setting. With live music and entertainment to serenade you through the night, this resort offers all the amenities and services to provide the special attention to the smallest of wedding details that every couple deserves.

LOCATION DETAILS: There are four wedding locations with no names. One is known as the formal location, a hill where the bride and groom face the ocean. Informal sites include a fairly public ocean-view location. The beach bluff area is a little spot overlooking the beach. Chairs are not an option at this location. The grotto near the pool is great for vow renewals. There is no ocean view and it is in the center of the hotel circle. A wedding arch, available at no charge, can be used at any location. Parking and restrooms are available.

GROUNDS FEES AND DEPOSITS: $300, of which $250 is a nonrefundable deposit to secure your wedding date. You may secure a site one month prior to the date. Earlier bookings are accepted only if you are staying at the resort. The balance must be paid at least seven days prior to your wedding day, at which time the entire grounds fee becomes nonrefundable. Rates are doubled for holidays. There are several packages to choose from, and some include accommodations at the resort.

Food and beverage: Must be provided by hotel
Wedding sites: Formal location, ocean-view location, beach bluff, the grotto
Public receptions: Naupaka Terrace Steak House, Driftwood Sandbar & Grille
Private receptions: Plumeria Room (semiprivate), Midori Room (twenty-person maximum), Orchid and Hibiscus rooms (fifty to seventy-five maximum), Jasmine Ballroom
Beach access: Nukoli'i Beach is nearby

Four Seasons Resort Lana'i at Manele Bay

1 Manele Bay Road
P.O. Box 631380
Lanai City, Lanai, HI 96763
808-565-2000
808-565-2483 (fax)
www.fourseasons.com/manelebay/

The Four Seasons Resort Lana'i at Manele Bay, formerly the Manele Bay Hotel, can help to create a wedding so magical that you may never want to leave the island. Its tasteful Hawaiian-themed décor, luxurious open spaces, fine dining, comfortable pool, world-famous spa, and incredible views of the Pacific spilling onto beaches of pearl white sand make this spot a secluded piece of heaven. In this unspoiled wonderland, you can choose from a selection of eight elegant garden settings, including one with a koi pond, blushing lotus flowers, and gentle waterfalls washing over black lava rock. Rest assured whatever setting you choose, the memories of your wedding here will last a lifetime.

LOCATION DETAILS: This hotel is magnificent. The resort is managed by Four Seasons Resorts, whose attention to detail along with flawless customer service makes this location all the more desirable. The Kama'aina Garden, Hawaiian Garden, Japanese Garden, Chinese Garden, and Bromeliad Garden are nestled in the inner courtyards. They are ideal for smaller weddings (three to fifteen guests). The Lu'au Gardens sit in a large grassy area surrounded by tropical foliage. The Plumeria Lawn is a spectacular ocean-view site near the pool and can also accommodate larger groups. There are a few cliffside locations situated on the

Challenge at Manele Golf Course (see the Remote Locations section later in this chapter). Whatever location you choose, I highly recommend staying at the resort for at least two nights so that you can fully enjoy the amenities it offers. Parking is available and restrooms can be used as dressing rooms.

GROUNDS FEES AND DEPOSITS: Wedding packages start at $5,700 and include limousine transportation to and from the airport or Manele Harbor, a modest photo package, dress and tuxedo pressing, a wedding certificate, and a special amenity basket. The entire package amount is due as a nonrefundable deposit in order to secure your date. Prices are subject to change at any time. You must secure your wedding date directly with this hotel.

Food and beverage: In-house only
Wedding sites: Plumeria Lawn, Japanese Garden, Hawaiian Garden, Kama'aina Garden, Chinese Garden, Bromeliad Garden, Lu'au Gardens, Challenge at Manele Golf Course
Public receptions: Ihilani Restaurant, Hulopo'e Court
Private receptions: Poolside, Plumeria Lawn, ballrooms; other venue requests are welcomed
Beach access: Hulopo'e Beach is a four-minute walk away

lana'i | resorts

The Lodge at Koele

P.O. Box 631380
Lanai City, Lanai, HI 96763
808-565-2000 or 800-321-4666
808-565-2483 (fax)
www.fourseasons.com/koele/preview

Situated in the dramatic uplands of Lana'i, The Lodge provides you with a peaceful retreat of infinite luxuries and breathtaking landscapes. Majestic ceilings, rock fireplaces, fine dining, a million-dollar miniature golf course, lawn bowling, skeet shooting, and horseback riding are a few of the many things that are sure to make your stay a memorable one. Set between mountains and coastlines, amid fragrant gardens and emerald forests, this location is perfect for couples seeking refined elegance and untouched natural splendor. Couples can choose from a variety of one-of-a-kind settings, including The Lodge at Koele gazebo, the Great Lawn, the Pineapple Fountain, and the Koele Gardens.

LOCATION DETAILS: This lodge is very impressive. Nestled in the mountain side of this remote island, the climate is cool most of the year. Yet its wedding sites make up for it. Done in a grand scale and unlike any others, the gazebo is surrounded by a large lagoon with paved pathways, a remote orchid house, and the beauty of the majestic hillside surrounding you. The Pineapple Fountain area near the lagoon is quaint yet uniquely designed with flower-covered trellises. The lawn and garden areas are very large, allowing this property to accommodate up to six hundred of the most discriminating guests. You must secure your wedding date directly with this hotel. Parking and restrooms are available.

GROUNDS FEES: Wedding packages start out at $5,700 and include limo transportation to and from the airport or Manele Harbor, a modest photo package, dress and tuxedo pressing, a wedding certificate, and a special amenity basket. The entire package amount is non-refundable and required to secure your date. Prices are subject to change at any time.

Food and beverage: In-house only
Wedding sites: Gazebo, Great Lawn, Pineapple Fountain, Koele Gardens
Public receptions: Terrace Restaurant, formal dining room
Private receptions: Pineapple Fountain, Great Lawn, several ballrooms; other venue requests are welcomed
Beach access: The closest beach is a thirty-minute drive

Maria Lanakila Catholic Church © A & C Photography

churches

churches

When you're thinking of a destination wedding, churches may not be your first choice. Still, one could provide you with the perfect option for a religious ceremony. One exceptional chapel ceremony at Grand Wailea's Seaside Chapel created a Hawaiian fairy tale wedding for a young couple from the East Coast. An emcee was hired to guide the guests to specific areas outside the chapel so they could enjoy a perfectly planned Hawaiian pre-processional. It began with a canoe arrival of men dressed in the traditional celebratory attire, paddling in on the lagoon behind the chapel. Blessings were chanted in the Hawaiian language as they made their way across the lagoon, disembarked, and proceeded to the entrance. As a conch shell blew in the distance, the guests were mesmerized by the loud, deep voice of the Hawaiian chanter as the men began to perform an authentic native dance. Guests were then escorted into the church and the processional began immediately afterwards with the bride trailing behind in all her splendor.

Hawai'i provides a numerous selection of churches to choose from, many of which are Roman Catholic. Nearly all the churches allow interfaith marriages, although some may require the minister or priest to meet with the couple prior to their special day. Catholic churches have specific requirements and an application process that takes about three months to process. Some smaller chapels provide a place of worship for those not belonging to an established church. Many churches in Hawai'i were built in the late 1800s and early 1900s, and several are listed as state and national historic sites. These elegant churches offer you the chance to wed in a tropical paradise while participating in a traditional church or chapel ceremony.

church bells

advantages

- Tradition blended with a tropical setting.

- Arrangements will be perfect regardless of weather.

- You can hear the ceremony well: No amplification is necessary.

things to consider

- The ceremony will be held indoors.

- Travel itineraries may not allow you to meet with a minister beforehand.

- No flower petals are allowed in any of the churches.

- Most churches have no direct beach access or sunset view.

- Alcohol is usually prohibited and the facilities are limited.

Keawala'i Church

190 Makena Road
Makena, Maui, HI 96753
808-879-5557
keawalai@maui.net

Keawala'i, an enchanting old Hawaiian church made of coral stone and lava rock, offers couples the chance to experience a truly special wedding. Located in the heart of Makena, this rural church is a historical religious site. A small cemetery lays prominantly off to the side of the church and is surrounded by lush green grass and native plumeria trees, allowing your wedding to be blessed by the spirits of old Maui. Cooled by trade winds from over the Pacific, this Protestant church can accommodate parties of two hundred or more and provides a private room where the bridal party can hide until its time for the processional to begin. The church staff is very involved and encourages couples to incorporate a bit of Hawai'i into their ceremony as well as traditional customs of the church. Bathroom facilities as well as an outdoor reception area are also at your disposal. The church interior is decorated with native woods and crisp white walls where a red curtain serves as a backdrop in the center of the altar. With a floor constructed of ohia wood and an altar made of koa and ulu—symbolizing eternal life—couples that wed here will feel the fullness of Hawai'i's tradition and legacy.

LOCATION DETAILS: There is a mandatory pre-ceremony meeting with the minister at the church so that a little of your lives can be incorporated into your ceremony. Please remember that there is a historic graveyard right next to the church. Wedding facilities are not available on Sundays and Mondays. There are strict guidelines as to decorating the interior of the church. No aisle runner is allowed; no tape is allowed to secure any decorations. Parking is available and an outdoor restroom is provided. Afterward you can hold your reception at the Maui Prince Resort, a two-minute drive, or the Seawatch Restaurant, a four-minute drive away.

GROUNDS FEES: $500 (includes the minister's fee). A $100 deposit is due at least ninety days prior to your wedding date, with the balance due on the wedding day. Deposit will be refunded if notification is given within forty-eight hours of your event.

Food and beverage: Outside caterers and nonalcoholic beverages are permitted
Public receptions: None
Private receptions: Lawn area, with contingencies
Beach access: Makena Beach is a two-minute walk down the road

Grand Wailea Seaside Chapel

3850 Wailea Alanui Drive
Wailea, Maui, HI 96753
808-875-1234 or 800-888-6100
www.grandwailea.com

With the warm Maui sunlight filtering through four stained-glass Hawaiian murals, couples can say "I do" amid an array of brilliant colors at the Grand Wailea Chapel. Among the most popular churches on Maui, the Grand Wailea Chapel is a sea of red oak floors, mahogany walls, and cherrywood pews. Its seventeenth-century chandelier and vaulted ceilings lend charm, and a koi lagoon and garden gazebos give it a romantic and intimate touch. Seating up to fifty guests, this chapel's elegance provides a perfect setting for the celebration of commitment.

LOCATION DETAILS: The chapel can bring in chairs to accommodate up to 125 guests. A burgundy carpet runs down the center aisleway. You can literally hear a pin drop due to the fantastic acoustics. One bonus feature is the ability to ring the chapel bells as you're exiting the church immediately after the ceremony. The chapel itself offers many picturesque photo opportunities. Parking is available and the restrooms can be used as dressing rooms. You have several choices for a public reception: The Humuhumunukunukuapua'a (named after our state fish) is the most authentic Hawaiian-style restaurant which can be found in the Grand Wailea Resort property. Bistro Molokini is an Italian restaurant near the pool and can accommodate moderately sized groups. Guests with an appetite for Asian fare will enjoy the Kincha Japanese restaurant. Other possibilities are nearby.

GROUNDS FEES AND DEPOSITS: $3,700 (for sunset ceremony), $3,200 (for daytime ceremony) for a 1.5-hour time slot. A 50 percent deposit is nonrefundable and has to be paid at time of booking. The remaining balance due thirty days prior to the ceremony. If cancellation or postponement occurs within two weeks of your date, 100 percent of the site fee or package will be charged—regardless of the reason, including inclement weather. The gratuity fees are currently 21 percent.

Food and beverage: In-house only
Public receptions: Humuhumunukunukuapua'a, Bistro Molokini, Kincha
Private receptions: Grand dining room, two chapel overlooks, oceanfront lawns, poolside venues, ballrooms
Beach access: Wailea Beach is nearby

The Honolua Chapel

Ritz-Carlton Kapalua
1 Ritz-Carlton Drive
Kapalua, Maui, HI 96761
808-669-6200 or 800-262-8440
www.ritzcarlton.com/resorts/kapalua

Located on the slopes of the West Maui Mountains at the Ritz-Carlton Kapalua is the Honolua Chapel. At one time, this little chapel was the only place of worship for the plantation community. Recently renovated, the inside has windows bordering the east wall; and a small stained-glass window etched with tropical flowers near the altar adds to its charm and style. The ceiling is tall, giving a spacious and open feel to the space. A small parish office can be used as a changing and waiting room for brides and attendants. With the advantage of being dedicated primarily to weddings, this private wedding chapel also has a grassy area with a gazebo. Limited parking and restrooms are available. Distant ocean views will enrich the memories of those who have their wedding ceremonies here.

LOCATION DETAILS: This chapel is quaint and intimate and one of my favorite churches on Maui. The chapel and gazebo are a two-minute drive from the lobby of the Ritz-Carlton and can comfortably seat up to sixty guests. You and your party can travel by horse and carriage, limousine service, or shuttles. Unique photo sites include a spectacular cliff, and you can arrange for a golf cart to take you there after the ceremony. There is no beach access; you will have to drive at least five minutes to get photos on the beach. Kapalua weather tends to be more rainy than in some other Maui locales, so be prepared for inclement weather. Options for your reception include the Banyan Tree at the Ritz-Carlton, and the Plantation House Restaurant.

GROUNDS FEES AND DEPOSITS: The Honolua Chapel, with gazebo, is $2,700. Packages start at $4,500. Availability is on a first-come, first-served basis. Fifty percent of the grounds fee is required as a nonrefundable deposit, with the remaining balance due thirty days prior to your event.

Food and beverage: Provided by the Ritz-Carlton
Public receptions: The Banyan Tree or the nearby Plantation House Restaurant
Private receptions: Many options at the Ritz-Carlton
Beach access: A ten-minute walk or a five-minute drive

St. John's Church

8992 Kula Highway
Kula, Maui, HI 96790
808-878-1485 or 808-878-6974
www.episcopalhawaii.org/churches/stjohn-kula

In a small pastoral area of Maui, there is a place called Keokea, where Chinese immigrant farmers once founded a church. Still sitting on the slopes of Mount Haleakala is the same structure that was first built in 1907 from wood pieces that floated in through Makena landing and were then transported up the mountainside by horse-drawn carts. With views of the Pacific and the West Maui Mountains, this location provides a perfect setting for a small wedding away from the hustle and bustle of the beachfront. The simplicity of the church is augmented by gorgeous flower arrangements and decorations that carry on the Chinese heritage from decades past. Quiet and peaceful, with an excellent staff to assist you with your wedding needs, St. John's provides a church and a lawn area (both for weddings) and a parish hall as well as outdoor areas for receptions of up to two hundred people. In the lush uplands of Kula, St. John's Episcopal Church will make your church wedding an elegant and unforgettable event.

LOCATION DETAILS: The church lawns are very large with magnificent coastal views. The weather is quite cool, which offers some relief from the warmer locations near the beach. The church will allow you to bring your own caterer in if you choose to stay at the church for your reception. No red rose petals are allowed inside the church. No nails, tape, or tacks are allowed in your altar setup or pew decorations. Candles are OK as long as they are in a glass container—these will nicely enhance the church's ambience. Adequate parking is available and restrooms and dressing rooms are located at the parish hall.

GROUNDS FEES AND DEPOSITS: The $600 grounds fee includes two hours of use for any of the wedding locations. There is an additional $100 fee for rehearsals (for a one-hour use). An on-site facilitator is included with the fees. A $50 non-refundable deposit secures your date. The remaining balance is due on or before your wedding day.

Food and beverage: Can be brought in
Public receptions: Kula Lodge (a fifteen-minute drive)
Private receptions: Parish hall, outdoor lawns
Beach access: None, but a thirty minute drive will take you to the North Shore

St. Theresa Catholic Church

25 West Lipoa Street
Kihei, Maui, HI 96753
808-879-2649
www.saint-theresa.com

The only Catholic Church on the south side of the island, St. Therea's Church dates back to 1928. Flowers from the islands decorate the stained glass windows along the side walls and a painting of the patroness of the church is imbedded in tiles on the wall, blessing the entrance way. Built in a near semi-circle the interior is large enough to seat 600. Tall ceilings with skylights and recently installed air conditioning create a pleasant atmosphere. Careful consideration was taken with the altar's décor with furnishings made from the endangered Koa tree and a massive crucifix carved from a large ohia log transferred from the Big Island. Every detail of St. Therea's Church is laced in history and meaning, making it the perfect venue for a Catholic ceremony in south Maui.

LOCATION DETAILS: This church is in the heart of Kihei, but you wouldn't know it once you're inside. Pew decorations are difficult to attach due to the unique style of the benches. The altar area is off limits to photographers, videographers, musicians and decorations. There is no ocean view. However, a miniature garden is available for photos in the back of the church. Ample parking and restrooms are available. The closest high-end options for the reception are in Wailea, a fifteen-minute drive away. A nice compromise is Marco's in Kihei, or Sarento's on the Beach and the Five Palms restaurant, which are located before you get into Wailea on South Kihci Road.

GROUNDS FEES AND DEPOSITS: $1,100, of which $1,000 is a nonrefundable deposit. The remaining $100 is payable to the priest and is due one month prior to your wedding day. In order to meet with the Catholic church's requirements you will need to contact your local parish priest and set up the required sessions and then submit the proper documents to the diocese in Honolulu. Please allow at least three months for the entire application process.

Food and beverage: Prohibited
Public receptions: Marco's, Sarento's, Five Palms
Private receptions: None
Beach access: None, but a fifteen minute drive will take you to scenic south Kihei and Wailea Beach.

Sacred Hearts Catholic Church

712 Wainee Street
Kapalua, Maui, HI 96761
808-661-0552

Distinguished by a set of gorgeous stained-glass windows that shower you with color-streaked rays of sunshine, Sacred Hearts Church is located on the west side of Maui in the Kapalua area. Nestled in the midst of Norfolk pines, you would never know you're on an island other than the crisp ocean air and gentle tradewinds that embrace the quaint Kapalua village area. Situated near the Ritz-Carlton and the Kapalua Bay Hotel you have access to some of the finest accommodations and reception venues nearby. Among its features are a gorgeous hand-carved altar, sliding doors that open on either side of the church to let the cool ocean breeze flow through, mahogany pews, and delicately laid tile flooring. Sacred Hearts history is rich in the community and its charming presence captivates your soul as you share the most intimate moments of your life with the one you love.

LOCATION DETAILS: This church location gives you a feeling that you're in the mountains with tall pine trees and a cooler climate. Being tucked away off the main road leading to the Ritz-Carlton, it's easy to miss if you're not looking. After the ceremony, couples often have their pictures taken within small grassy areas that provide a small garden setting as a backdrop and then drive to the ocean for beachside photos while guests make their way to the cocktail reception. Parking is available with outdoor restrooms.

GROUNDS FEES AND DEPOSITS: $1,100, of which $1,000 is a nonrefundable deposit. The remaining $100 is payable to the priest and is due one month prior to your wedding day. In order to meet with the church's requirements contact your local parish priest and set up the required sessions and then he will help you submit the proper documents to the diocese in Honolulu. Please allow at least three months for the entire application process.

Food and beverage: Prohibited
Public receptions: Ritz-Carlton Kapalua, Plantation House Restaurant
Private receptions: None
Beach access: None. Closest beach is a five or more minute drive

Maria Lanakila Catholic Church

712 Wainee Street
Lahaina, Maui, HI 96761
808-661-0552

With the support of American and French citizens, Maria Lanakila was the first Catholic Church built on the island of Maui in 1856, with a larger building dedicated in 1858. As the sugarcane industry took off in the 1860s, bringing with it the arrival of Portuguese and Filipino laborers, Catholicism soon became the largest denomination in Hawai'i. The influence of French cathedrals and their long, sweeping columns and Gothic steeples is apparent throughout the structure. This grand Roman Catholic cathedral is located in the heart of Lahaina town, yet away from daydreaming beachgoers. Graceful beauty surrounds you as you make your way inside where tall pillars line the isle way leading up to an impressive altar. More narrow than most churches, tasteful colors and light accents create the perfect atmosphere for a small and intimate ceremony.

LOCATION DETAILS: There is a small garden area at the back for limited photos and video after the ceremony. The church itself is very pretty with vaulted ceilings and tasteful décor. Most clients use two locations to give them more photography and videography opportunities. A graveyard is located nearby yet is somewhat protected from foot traffic. Restrooms are available, and parking is found across the street. For your reception, consider Pacific'O and I'o Restaurant, the closest venues that are used to accommodating wedding clients. There is also the Lahaina Store Grille and Oyster Bar's rooftop location. Restaurants in Ka'anapali would be the next choice and may be perfect if you're staying on the Ka'anapali Coast.

GROUNDS FEES AND DEPOSITS: $1,100, of which $1,000 is a nonrefundable deposit. The remaining $100 is payable to the priest and is due one month prior to your wedding day. In order to meet with the church's requirements you will need to contact your local parish priest and set up the required sessions and then submit the proper documents to the diocese in Honolulu.

Food and beverage: Prohibited
Public receptions: Pacific'O, I'o Restaurant, Lahaina Store Grille, Oyster Bar
Private receptions: None
Beach access: None. Closest beach worthy of the occassion is located at 505 Front Street less than five minutes away

Chapel by the Sea

3610 Rice Street
Lihue, Kauai, HI 96766
808-245-5071 or 800-246-5620

Resting atop the tranquil waters of Kaua'i Lagoons is the Chapel by the Sea. With a sun-soaked interior, and double doors on each side that open to allow the trade winds to pass through, Chapel by the Sea is the ultimate location for a private indoor ceremony. The chapel is tucked away on the outer edge of Kaua'i Lagoons, so it is very easy to miss your turnoff. Make your way just past the Kaua'i Marriott and take a sharp right at a small sign designating the way to the chapel. You'll pass a string of houses surrounded by rolling hills and a sweeping ocean view and then travel up a gentle hill until you catch your first glimpse of the octagon shaped chapel. Pink hues can be seen on the exterior while a crisp heavenly white adorns the interior. This venue naturally sets a breathtaking scene as the bride makes her way down the isle. Overlooking the Nawiliwili Harbor, the Chapel by the Sea is the perfect setting for a traditional chapel wedding in Hawai'i.

LOCATION DETAILS: This location is managed by the Kaua'i Marriott Resort, which is also the closest option for an intimate reception dinner. The chapel appears to be floating in the lagoon, with a bridge entrance leading to the chapel itself. There is a sixty-person maximum capacity, with forty-eight comfortable chairs. Transportation may be necessary for you and your guests and can be provided by the resort. A white wedding carriage is also available as a fun form of transportation. Keep in mind there are no restrooms and only limited parking.

GROUNDS FEES AND DEPOSITS: Fees vary per time of day, from $2,700 (10:00 a.m.) to $2,900 (1:00 p.m.) and $3,100 (4:30 p.m.). Included are chairs fitted with white covers and brocade sashes, and six aisle stanchions decorated with white tulle. There is an option to add two nights in a deluxe ocean-view room and daily breakfast for two by adding $600 to the site fee. A $500 nonrefundable deposit is required to secure your date, with the balance due thirty days prior. Certain holidays are subject to an additional $500 fee. There is also a $250 rehearsal site fee when applicable.

Food and beverage: In-house only
Public receptions: Terrace Restaurant at the Kaua'i Lagoons
Private receptions: Kaua'i Marriott Resort
Beach access: None. The Kaua'i Marriott Resort's beach is a five minute drive

Church of the Pacific

P.O. Box 223154
Princeville, Kauai, HI 96722
808-826-6481 or 808-828-6772 (pastor)
Hours: Monday-Friday, 1 p.m. to 3 p.m.
info@church-of-the-pacific.org
www.church-of-the-pacific.org

Located in an area that was once nothing but guava trees, the beautiful sand-stone Church of the Pacific sits on the gentle slopes of Princeville on Kaua'i. Here couples have the choice of either an indoor church wedding—under beautiful stained-glass windows with the sun filtering in through either side of the church—or an outdoor gazebo wedding that provides you with faraway views of the Hanalei Bay. On meticulously maintained grounds atop rolling hills, couples can also have their reception in the church's large community hall. Mauve, red, and white decorate the interior with a very spacious atmosphere. Comfortable chair seating (vs. pews) give your guests the opportunity to experience a traditional church wedding on one of the most beautiful islands in the Pacific.

LOCATIONS DETAILS: This location is well cared for with beautifully manicured grounds. Some uneven ground around the gazebo makes it a challenge to place chairs. There is a clear, open view of the sky all around the gazebo, making this location feel spiritual. The property sits high enough above the highway that you're removed from any noise disturbances. Your options are unlimited for receptions, as the venue can accommodate both indoor and outdoor events.

The Princeville Resort is the closest upscale dining option and is a ten-minute drive away. If you choose to marry in the church, then you have to use the church's minister or another licensed minister. Forty people can be seated in front of the gazebo. The church seats 140. There is plenty of parking, and a changing room and restroom are combined with a small nursery.

GROUNDS FEES AND DEPOSITS: $150, which includes the minister at the church; $70 for two hours at the gazebo. It's an extra $35 an hour for the gazebo. There is no deposit required in order to secure your date.

Food and beverage: BYO, through a licensed caterer
Public receptions: Princeville Resort
Private receptions: Privately catered event on the property
Beach access: None. Hanalei Bay is a twenty-minute drive away

St. Sylvester Catholic Church

Sister church of St. Catherine and St. William
5021-A Kawaihayu Road
Kapaa, Kauai, HI 96746
808-822-7900
Hours: Monday–Friday, 8:30 a.m. to 2:30 p.m.
www.stcatherinekauai.org

Situated within the busy town of Kilauea, this uniquely shaped church sits quietly off to the side atop a gently sloped hill. By taking the same road that leads you to the famous Kilauea Lighthouse, you will find this church directly past Kilauea School, set back from the road and surrounded by tall wiliwili trees that provide a quiet oasis away from the hustle and bustle of town. There are many entrances to this circular shaped church. Made out of lava rock and wood, the interior seats your guest on pews that have been strategically placed in a circle. Natural wood framing and oak colored wood tones create a warm and inviting setting as you pronounce your vows on a raised center altar. With exceptionally beautiful frescoes of the Station of the Cross (painted by famous local artist Jean Charlot), this location provides you with a one-of-a-kind church wedding location.

LOCATION DETAILS: Sunday services are held at 8:30 a.m. This church is about five minutes off the highway. It's up on a hill in an area all on its own, surrounded by trees and bushes, so it's sheltered from all the busy town traffic. This untraditional Catholic church is shaped in an octagon with a cone shaped roof. The small wooden pews can comfortably seat 150. There are no offices or reception hall. There are other restrictions that should be taken under consideration; these can be found on the Web site. There is adequate parking but no restrooms. The closest options for a private reception are in Princeville, which is a twenty-minute drive away. The Princeville Resort offers upscale dining. CJ's Steak and Seafood is available for a public reception.

GROUNDS FEES: A $50 donation is requested to reserve the church for your wedding day. This donation is refundable if a cancellation occurs.

Food and beverage: Prohibited
Public receptions: Princeville restaurants and CJ's Steak and Seafood
Private receptions: Princeville Resort
Beach access: None. Closest beach is a twenty-five minute drive away

Wai'oli Hui'ia Church

5-5393A Kuhio Highway
Hanalei, Kauai, HI 96714
808-826-6253
Hours: Tuesday, Wednesday, Thursday, 9:30 a.m. to 1:00 p.m.

Set in the heart of Hanalei, where the majority of Hawai'i's taro plants are grown, the Wai'oli Hui'ia Church, built in 1912, reflects the American Gothic architectural style so popular in New England at the time. The bell tower of this shingle-roofed church houses the old mission bell from the Wai'oli Hui'ia Mission Museum that sits at the back of the property. Founded by New England missionaries, this church is listed on the state and national registers of historic places, and it preserves the traditions of old Hawai'i, with Sunday services still held in both English and Hawaiian. Surrounded by the laughter of children playing on the soccer fields and basketball court nearby, couples can wed in an old plantation-style setting that stands as a reminder of decades past. Under beautiful stained-glass windows shaded by magnificent areca palms, you will experience a truly Hawaiian-style wedding.

LOCATION DETAILS: The surrounding taro fields and emerald green mountains provide a stunning backdrop for photos. The environment is comfortable, with no immediate distractions, as the church is set on its own grounds rather than being in the middle of a busy town. This church allows you to plan a traditional Hawaiian-style church wedding at one of the most desirable locations on the north shore of Kaua'i. Plenty of parking and restrooms are available. A public reception can be held at Sushi Blues in Hanalei, which offers Pacific Rim dining and can accommodate larger crowds. Hanalei is a five-minute drive away.

GROUNDS FEES AND DEPOSITS: $450 site fee. The church is available for weddings only on Tuesdays, Wednesdays, Thursdays, and Saturdays. A $250 fee is also collected for the pastor (the church prefers that you use its pastor). A $50 refundable deposit is required to secure your wedding date. There is a 250-person maximum at this location.

Food and beverage: Prohibited
Public receptions: Sushi Blues
Private receptions: Princeville Resort
Beach access: None. Closest beach is a ten-minute drive away

© Mike Sydney

remote locations

remote locations

You have to have somewhat of an adventurous spirit when considering a remote location. It's most likely that some of the details that are important to most may not be as important to someone getting married in an out-of-the way place. It's quite possible that you will arrive wrinkled, be rained on, have your hair go wild, or get red dirt on your dress, all in the process of getting there. When you choose a remote location, getting to and from the special place itself—together with the reason you're going in the first place—will constitute a unique experience. I remember one couple that truly created their own storybook wedding by selecting a remote waterfall as their wedding location. Two limos picked everyone up at their hotel and brought them to the heliport where three private helicopters were standing by. It was early morning on New Years Day and it was amazing that no one panicked over the inclement weather we were having. After learning that Maui County closed the heliport to the general public, I looked for my pilot to perform a miracle. With a little patience, everyone was finally whisked away to a remote location on the other side of the island. The weather prevented all three helicopters from landing at the base of the waterfall, yet we were able to land on a lava rock bluff at the edge of the ocean which was out of this world. The couple pronounced their vows with ten of their closest family and friends in attendance as the pounding surf surrounded them. You may want to ask yourself if you have the ability to go with the flow, no matter what the journey entails. If you do, then the following locations will truly allow you to create a once-in-a-lifetime experience, unlike any other.

faraway fantasy

advantages

- You can plan a unique, custom-made ceremony.

- You can maintain your privacy.

- It offers a once-in-a-lifetime experience.

things to consider

- No facilities, no restrooms, and no running water will be available.

- Brides should consider nontraditional attire or opt to pack their traditional dress and then change once they arrive at the location.

- You should be prepared for unpredictable weather conditions.

- Vendors will charge more for remote locations due to the extra time involved.

remote locations

Hui Aloha Church

Mary Jane and Charles Kahaleauki
H.C. Box 233
Hana, Kaupo, Maui, HI 96713
808-248-8209

Hui Aloha Church can be reached only by a two- to three-hour drive to an extremely primitive area with nothing but lush tropical rainforest and sweeping grasslands set against majestic cliffs. Built in 1838, this church stands as a reminder of an age that has since passed. With aged wooden pews and altar, and stucco walls both inside and out, the church comfortably seats fifty. White with brown shingles, it is easily spotted from a few miles away as you drive there along the coastline. This site is popular for proposals, with couples then returning to marry at a later date. Located on the back side of the island in the small town of Kaupo, Hui Aloha Church is the ultimate destination for a remote church location.

LOCATION DETAILS: This remote location tends to be extremely windy. Far away from civilization as we know it, you must bring in all your own amenities. Vendors charge much more due to the lengthy drive time involved. Limited parking is available, and no restrooms.

GROUNDS FEE: A $100 donation and a $100 cleaning fee are required to secure your wedding date.

Food and beverage: BYO
Public receptions: Hotel Hana Maui and Hana Ranch Restaurant
Private receptions: Hotel Hana Maui and Plantation House
Beach access: Closest white sand beach is in Hana town, a thirty-minute drive away

Hamoa Beach

Two and a half miles from the Hotel Hana Maui (a seven-minute drive)

Hamoa Beach, one of the much less traveled beaches, is the only white-sand coastline in the little town of Hana. The weather is much more favorable during the summer months on this densely forested side of the island. Getting to it proves to be rather challenging. Travel time may be up to three to four hours by car. You can also hire a private airplane that will get you there in only twenty-five minutes. Frequented mostly by guests of Hotel Hana Maui, the beach is less crowded on weekdays than weekends, when local fishermen are in search of the ultimate catch. After a relatively steep walk down to the beach, couples can enjoy a ceremony of their dreams at one of the most private beach locations on Maui. There are restrooms and limited roadside parking is available.

LOCATION DETAILS: Hamoa Beach is the only accessible white-sand beach on the east side of the island. The Hotel Hana Maui offers a nearby pavilion for a fee as long as you're staying at the hotel. Vendors will charge you extra because of the drive time involved. You must bring in all of your own amenities. If you decide to hold a reception, the closest venues are the Hotel Hana Maui and its Main Dining Room restaurant, and the Hana Ranch Restaurant in the town of Hana, open on Wednesday, Friday, and Saturday evenings only.

GROUNDS FEE: None

Food and beverage: BYO
Public receptions: Hotel Hana Maui, Hana Ranch Restaurant
Private receptions: Hotel Hana Maui
Beach access: Down a steep hill or winding staircase

Polihale Beach

Polihale State Park, West Kaua'i
1.5 hour drive from Lihu'e Airport

Miles from civilization and accessible only by a long and bumpy sugarcane road, Polihale Beach is often overlooked. Empty and unspoiled, the beaches and sand dunes of Polihale offer miles of staggering physical beauty. A favorable destination for sun seekers, this beach is known for its dry climate. You will bask in the air of the softest of golden sunsets as you feel the essence and beauty of old Hawai'i. Remaining even today is the heiau (Hawaiian temple) at Polihale, one of the oldest and most sacred in Hawai'i. Known for its spiritual serenity, Polihale will fascinate and delight you as few other places do.

LOCATION DETAILS: This beach is definitely for adventurous thrill seekers. The weather can be a bit unpredictable, so a four-wheeled drive vehicle is recommended for travel. There are absolutely no services available, so this location will give you the experience of being wed in isolation from the world itself. There is parking wherever you can find a spot, but there are no restrooms. The closest town for any reception you might want to hold is Kehaka, nearly twelve miles away.

GROUNDS FEE: None

Food and beverage: BYO
Public receptions: None
Private receptions: None
Beach access: Direct

Fern Grotto

Smith's Tropical Paradise
174 Wailua Road
Kapaa, Kauai, HI 96746
808-821-6887 or 808-821-6888
www.smithskauai.com
smiths@aloha.net

For an especially memorable Hawaiian experience, cruise up the Wailua River to a lava-rock grotto and say your vows under a canopy of tropical ferns actually growing upside down from the roof of the grotto. In ancient times the Fern Grotto was once off limits to all but Hawaiian royalty, who believed that standing in the interior of the cave, while listening to the resonating sounds of Hawaiian musicians, was a sacred blessing. Now, serenaded by native birds and cooled by the mists of a waterfall, couples can wed in a geological phenomenon that will show you why Kaua'i has adopted the name "The Garden Isle." The dewy emerald grotto surrounds couples with native Hawaiian plants and an array of colors that provide a rainforest-type atmosphere. After a simple riverboat trip up the historic and sacred Wailua River, couples can say "I do" amid tropical grasslands as the cloud-capped Mount Waialeale rises in the background.

LOCATION DETAILS: A private boat can take you up the Wailua River to the Fern Grotto area, departing at 8:30 a.m., 11:45 a.m., 3:45 p.m., or 4:00 p.m. You will travel upstream and arrive at your destination in approximately forty-five minutes. Boats operate every day. The journey itself is definitely more adventurous than elegant. Simple wedding attire is the way to go. Another option is to have your wedding in the garden (see the listing for Wailua Tropical Gardens—East Side in the "Gardens" section, page 44) and take a public cruise up to the Fern Grotto afterward, where a musician will sing you the "Hawaiian Wedding Song" once you're there. A Hawaiian luau is held on the property on Mondays, Wednesdays, and Fridays beginning at 6:30 p.m. The closest town for a private reception is Lihu'e. There are restrooms and plenty of parking.

GROUNDS FEES AND DEPOSITS: Fern Grotto wedding packages start at $700 and include the boat (up to eighteen persons, maximum), a musician, your minister, and two flower leis. Full payment is required to secure your wedding date and time. With advance notice, marriage licenses can be issued by the general manager.

Food and beverage: BYO
Public receptions: Luau on Monday, Wednesday, or Friday evenings
Private receptions: None
Beach access: None

12th and 17th Holes at Challenge at Manele

Four Seasons Resort at Manele Bay
1233 Fraser Avenue
Lanai City, Lanai, HI 96763
808-565-2222
www.fourseasons.com/lanai/

From the Four Seasons at Manele Bay Hotel, a five-minute drive will take you to the clubhouse where you will then need to take a short ride in a golf cart to get to either of these locations. Laid out on some of the most dramatic sea cliffs in all of Hawai'i, the Challenge at Manele Golf Course offers you the chance for an outdoor wedding set amid a tropical wonder with modern comforts just ten minutes away. This meticulously maintained course surrounds you with lush flowing hills of jade green that outline the lava rock's edge. Couples have the choice of either hole 12 or hole 17.

LOCATION DETAILS: This is the most dramatic cliffside location in the state of Hawai'i. What makes this location remote is the different forms of transportation it requires for you to get there. You are limited to a late afternoon start time so that your event doesn't conflict with the golf course clientele. Parking and restrooms are available at the clubhouse. The clubhouse can also accommodate a private party for your reception, or you can choose the Four Seasons as your next closest option.

GROUNDS FEE: The practice tee box and 12 and 17th tees have to have special approval from the director of conference services at Castle & Cooke Resorts. Custom quotes are given to individual clients based on their specific needs.

Food and beverage: In-house only
Public receptions: Four Seasons at Manele Bay
Private receptions: Challenge at Manele Bay clubhouse, Four Seasons and Manele Bay
Beach access: None. Closest beach is a five-minute drive away from the clubhouse

Sweetheart (Pu'u Pehe) Rock

A three-minute drive south from the Manele Harbor in Lana'i

To the north of Hulopo'e Beach, just offshore, is Pu'u Pehe Rock, also known as Sweetheart Rock. It contains a history laced with romance, love, misery, and sadness. Legend states that Pu'u Pehe, a young girl from Maui, was captured by a young warrior from Lana'i. Stunned by her beauty, the young warrior feared losing her to other suitors, leading him to hide her in a sea cave near the rock. One day, he returned to find that she had drowned with the rising tide. Overrun with grief, the young warrior retrieved her body and buried it on the eighty-foot-high rock island. He then leapt from Pu'u Pehe Rock to his untimely death, hoping that he might meet Pu'u Pehe's soul in the world beyond earth and time.

LOCATION DETAILS: It is a bit tricky to get to the rock without walking a great distance via a lava-rock trail. You will definitely need good shoes. If you rent a Jeep, you can drive along the coastline and then park and walk out to the area where you want to wed. The legendary Sweetheart Rock will be the main backdrop for your entire ceremony, making this a very special remote location. There is limited parking and there are no restrooms. Four Seasons Resort at Manele Bay, a five-minute drive away, can provide you with a variety of options for a reception.

GROUNDS FEE: None

Food and beverage: BYO
Public receptions: None
Private receptions: Four Seasons at Manele
Beach access: None. Hulapoe Beach is a ten minute hike away

Kaiolohia Bay/Shipwreck Beach

Thirty-minute drive from The Lodge at Koele

On Lana'i's northeast shore is an eight-mile stretch of sand known as Shipwreck Beach. Many ships have met their watery demise in the powerful currents and numerous reefs of the Kalohi Channel. Perhaps the most famous resident on this beach is a World War II Liberty ship, whose rusted hulk still clings to a reef near shore, although this particular wreckage was not the result of an accident. The vessel was given "anchorage" here after World War II as an economical means of disposal. Made of concrete, it has withstood the ocean currents for more than fifty years. Wild and beautiful with an array of sun-kissed sand, lava rock and boulders, and unexpected scenery, Shipwreck Beach is a favorite among the locals and is sure to become a favorite of yours.

LOCATION DETAILS: If you're up for an adventure ride to a historic beach on a remote Hawaiian island then this may be an option for you. There are absolutely no amenities once you leave The Lodge at Koele, so you must pack everything in. You can either drive yourself or rent transportation. It will take about thirty minutes from The Lodge at Koele. The climate is unpredictable because the beach lies between the Lana'i and Molokai channels. There is parking available but there are no restrooms.

GROUNDS FEES: None

Food and beverage: BYO
Public receptions: None
Private receptions: None
Beach access: Direct

© Bill Stockwell

restaurants

restaurants

R estaurants are a wonderful venue not only for a reception but also for an intimate bridal party luncheon, rehearsal dinner parties, and more. The Islands host a variety of restaurants, offering everything from Pacific Rim and Asian fare to rustic dishes and Italian classics. It's always best to research restaurant options after your wedding location is determined. That way you can choose from the restaurants located nearby. The next step to narrow down your options is to select the type of cuisine you'd like to have, the type of atmosphere you're looking for (open air, fun and lively, elegant and formal, indoor or outdoor), and the price range, if any. I find service is also an important issue to most clients. Keep in mind that during your research you may find a few restaurants have wedding venues on their property and may offer to help you with the planning process if you select their site. You also can hire an independent wedding coordinator to plan the event at that particular restaurant. I have picked some of the top restaurants on each of the three islands in this chapter with other suggestions listed afterwards (as well as in previous sections of the book). Each restaurant has their own policies regarding deposits, buy outs and menu options which is why it is important to decide who your reception planner will be prior to securing the venue for your event.

restaurant receptions

advantages

- Independent restaurants are more flexible than those in resorts, and some have special reception menus. Setup fees and prices are generally lower.

- Some restaurants offer rooms that allow you more privacy while still being served by the restaurant staff.

- There are restaurants that allow you to bring your own musicians, and some even allow you to bring in a DJ or small band.

things to consider

- You are seated with other patrons unless you reserve the entire facility, which is quite expensive.

- The cuisine preparations vary and sometimes a long time can pass between courses.

- Other patrons are close by so the service staff will have to be shared.

Spago

Four Seasons Resort Maui
3900 Wailea Alanui Drive
Wailea, Maui, HI 96753
808-879-2999
www.wolfgangpuck.com/rest/fine/spago/maui

Sophisticated yet relaxed, Spago is one of Wolfgang Puck's famous restaurants. The Asian-inspired interior here includes unique stone and woods, custom lighting, and exotic glass and art pieces. This restaurant has an intimate lounge area and bar, with a private dining room for special events. Guests can enjoy panoramic views of the Pacific Ocean and the Wailea Beach with a sunset unlike any you've ever seen. Spago utilizes the finest local ingredients, fusing Hawaiian and California cuisine, embracing traditional Island culinary techniques and offering Wolfgang Puck classics. Providing both family comforts and romantic evenings, Spago offers both indoor and outdoor lanai dining.

LOCATIONS DETAILS: Whether you're planning an intimate affair for two or a gala reception for a few hundred, Spago offers a variety of dining options. You can choose from a private dining room to the entire restaurant, which can be made available for a private breakfast, lunch, or evening event. Dinner is served nightly from 5:30 to 9:30, and reservations are recommended. Clients have the option to bring in their own live entertainment. The dress code is resort wear. Parking is by valet only.

Humuhumunukunukuapua'a

Grand Wailea Resort
3850 Wailea Alanui Drive
Wailea, Maui, HI 96753
808-875-1234, ext. 4900
www.grandwailea.com

This restaurant set in the beautiful Grand Wailea Hotel offers the freshest of tropical fish and seafood. Named after Hawaiian Islands' state fish, this Polynesian thatched-roof restaurant sits on a saltwater lagoon filled with a variety of local fish. After walking across a picturesque wooden bridge to enter the restaurant, couples sit at Hawaiian-style wooden tables while gazing at the tropical wonders on the meticulously maintained grounds of the Grand Wailea. Relaxing with the gently swaying palm trees, couples relish the experience of a romantic dinner in paradise.

LOCATIONS DETAILS: A large saltwater fish tank serves as the main focal point when you enter this restaurant. Low lighting and wood tones create a warm atmosphere in this one-of-a-kind Hawaiian-themed venue. This restaurant is open nightly at 5:30 for dinner, and seating areas can be created to easily accommodate two hundred people. Live music is provided in the early evenings on certain days of the week. The dress code is casual, but resort wear is recommended.

Seawatch

100 Wailea Golf Club Drive
Wailea, Maui, HI 96753
808-875-8080
www.seawatchrestaurant.com

Seawatch offers exquisite cuisine under the Wailea sun and stars, with the possibility of on-site weddings. Ceremonies can be held at the Upper Wedding Knoll, the Lower Wedding Knoll, and the Molokini Lookout, each with its own unique surroundings that tap into the Island lifestyle that many become so easily accustomed to. With an expansive interior and dining areas that flow gently into one another, this restaurant creates an inviting ambience enveloped by majestic palms and island flora. Seawatch effortlessly maintains a balance between fine dining and the casual lifestyle that Hawai'i is known for. Couples can enjoy classic dishes such as filet mignon or New York steaks, or local favorites like miso prawns and fresh fish caught daily in Hawaiian waters.

LOCATIONS DETAILS: High ceilings, colorful art, and beautiful furniture create a gorgeous setting for any occasion at this independently owned and operated restaurant. It can accommodate groups of 125, and is available for breakfast, lunch, and dinner. You can also rent out the entire restaurant for a completely exclusive event. Dining options include the outdoor lower lawn, a lanai area off to the side of general seating, or the inner restaurant area. Set menus are required for all parties of fifteen or more. Under certain circumstances, the restaurant allows clients to bring in live musicians for their entertainment. The dress code is casual, but resort wear is recommended. More information about ceremonies at Molokini Lookout can be found on page 36.

Nick's Fishmarket

Fairmont Kea Lani Maui
4100 Wailea Alanui Drive
Wailea, Maui, HI 96753
808-879-7224
www.tri-star-restaurants.com

Combining the magical beauty of Maui with the romantic flair of the Mediterranean, Nick's Fishmarket, located at the spectacular Fairmont Kea Lani Resort and Spa, offers the finest local and seafood cuisine. Guests outdoors will be captivated by overhead vine-covered trellises overflowing with blossoming flowers and sparkling lights, while guests indoors bask in the warmth and coziness of the main dining room. Rich earth tones and crisp white curves enhance the architecture. Diners look out over the lush grounds of the Kea Lani Hotel and the most gorgeous of tropical beaches are only a few minutes away—perfect for an elegant afterdinner stroll.

LOCATIONS DETAILS: Dark hues and tiki torch lighting provide a cozy atmosphere. For the connoisseurs, there is an incredible wine cellar on-site, and clients can choose to seat their guests in the main dining room, outdoors on the lanai, or in the private dining room located off to the side of the restaurant. Nick's Fishmarket can comfortably accommodate seventy-five guests. Set menus are required for all parties of twenty or more. Clients are allowed to bring in low-key live music for their entertainment if they choose the private dining room as their venue.

Plantation House Restaurant

2000 Plantation Club Drive
Lahaina, Maui, HI 96761
808-669-6299
www.theplantationhouse.com

High above Maui's coastline sits the Plantation House Restaurant. With an elegant blend of traditional plantation-style atmosphere, old-fashioned Hawaiian hospitality, and the finest of Island cuisine, the Plantation House has earned its fabulous reputation. The restaurant is located on the Plantation Golf Course at Kapalua and offers several unique locations for those wishing to have their wedding receptions there. Among them are the Main Dining Room, the Grille Room, and the Lower Lawn with variety of seating arrangements for up to 150 guests. Group tables can be reserved and arranged with all the trimmings needed to make your reception a special occasion.

LOCATIONS DETAILS: This restaurant is a sister restaurant to the Seawatch in Wailea and the décor was recently updated. There is a fireplace in the center of the dining room and an upper raised area that can be used for dining or serve as a stage or dance floor. The Grille Room is a perfect gathering spot for more private gatherings overlooking the stunning Kapalua landscape. With sweeping views of the dramatic Kapalua coastline, the Lower Lawn is an exceptional location for cocktails prior to dinner. You may also choose to rent out the entire restaurant for an exclusive event. Open for breakfast, lunch, and dinner, the menus are flexible yet center on hearty Hawaiian cuisine. The dress code is casual, but resort wear is recommended.

Pacific'O

505 Front Street
Lahaina, Maui, HI 96761
808-667-4341
www.pacificomaui.com

On one of Maui's sunniest beaches is an oasis of contemporary Pacific cuisine. At Pacific'O restaurant, a staff of seasoned professionals is committed to making your wedding reception something uniquely yours. Using the freshest and finest ingredients, Pacific'O restaurant provides many exciting dishes from around the islands in an exceptional oceanside setting. This restaurant offers fresh-caught fish, delicious organic fruits and vegetables, and spectacular presentations just steps from the water's edge. With attentive aloha-style service, this open-air restaurant presents such award-winning items as the catch of the day seared with a macadamia coconut crust and Thai peanut coconut sauce. Pacific'O restaurant is sure to be one of the most memorable experiences of your wedding day.

LOCATIONS DETAILS: One hundred and forty seats are available in this open-air restaurant with preset menus available for parties of twenty or more. Open seven days a week for lunch from 11:30 a.m. to 4:00 p.m., and dinner from 5:30 p.m., with the last seating at 9:00 p.m. Beige and white décor create a light and lively atmosphere, and a live jazz band is provided in the restaurant on Friday and Saturday evenings from 9:00 to midnight. Reservations are highly recommended. You have the option of reserving the entire restaurant, the inside area, or the outdoor lanai. Other dining options include the Ikena room, a private dining room upstairs, which seats up to one hundred, and the IO restaurant next door, which seats up to 120. The dress code is fun and casual.

Beach House Restaurant

5022 Lawai Road
Koloa, Kauai, HI 96756
808-742-1424
www.the-beach-house.com

Just a step away from the water's edge near Spouting Horn Beach is the Beach House Restaurant, a multilevel structure that offers several dining options. This restaurant gains its fame by gracefully melding together gracious Hawaiian service with innovative Pacific Rim cuisine and creative twists on Island favorites made with fresh local ingredients. With its breathtaking views, this restaurant provides the perfect tropical setting for a reception. Couples can reserve either part of the restaurant or the entire restaurant for up to two hundred guests. Venue areas include the lawn, the Lower Surf Lanai, the Gallery, and the Lower Surf. The lawn is large and can be used for both weddings and receptions.

LOCATIONS DETAILS: Affiliated with the Seawatch and Plantation House restaurants on Maui, the Beach House is all about the view. The Lower Surf, on the lower level, provides enough space for parties of up to forty people. The Lower Surf Lanai is an open-air setting with a seating capacity of just thirty-two. Located in the upper dining level of the restaurant, the Gallery offers a semiprivate place for intimate receptions with seating for up to thirty people. Some setup fees may apply for a bar on the lawn areas. Open for dinner, the dining room hours are from 5 p.m. to 10 p.m., seven days a week, all year round. Menus can be customized to fit any dietary needs. Live entertainment requests are gladly taken but must be preapproved. This venue is very popular so reservations are highly recommended. The dress code is resort wear. The Beach House also offers off-site catering services.

Gaylord's

3-2087 Kaumuali'i Highway
Lihue, Kauai, HI 96766
808-245-5608 or 808-245-9593
www.gaylordskauai.com

Located in the historical Wilcox home at Kilohana Plantation, this restaurant stands as a reminder of the days when sugarcane production dominated the island. Gaylord's can create the perfect ambience for both a romantic wedding and a reception. This large estate resembles an older English manor accented with Hawaiian details. A grand foyer marks the entrance, and an outdoor U-shaped patio setting with a grass courtyard in the center creates a protected area that's perfect for candle-lit dinners. The remaining rooms, and even the bathrooms, have been converted into mini stores with individual owners. Old plantation-style buildings and well-kept gardens serve as the backdrop as horse-drawn carriages saunter by in a distance. It can open up the Kilohana living room, a sitting room, a carriage house, or vast white tents. However, the simplest dining option is available within Gaylord's private dining room, which accommodates groups of up to forty on a moonlit patio. Gaylord's enticing menu combines fresh herbs and vegetables with out-of-the-ordinary fare such as venison and lamb.

LOCATIONS DETAILS: Open for breakfast, lunch, and dinner, Gaylord's can entertain parties as small as two or large as a thousand. Tents, custom menus, and entertainment are a few of the many services available. Dining options include the restaurant itself or the grassy area next to the estate. It also holds luaus on Tuesday and Thursdays. The dress code is casual to formal depending on the occasion.

The Terrace Restaurant at Kaua'i Lagoons

3351 Hoolaulea Way
Lihue, Kauai, HI 96766
808-241-6080

The Terrace Restaurant sits on the 750 acres of lush grasslands that make up the famous Kaua'i Lagoons Golf Course. Its European architecture lends a romantic ambience to this corner of the world. Located a mere five minutes from Lihu'e Airport and Nawiliwili Harbor, the Terrace offers you an opportunity to have your wedding and reception in the same place: The Chapel by the Sea (see page 102) is just beyond the lagoon. The main dining room is located in the center of the building and the bar is located off to the side, making it easy to have your cocktails in a separate area. The indoor/outdoor setting offers private dining in the evening amidst a tropical landscape that includes a lagoon, palm trees, flowers, and unique sculptures. Wood-framed doors with glass panels open to terraced-style seating for smaller groups. The cuisine at this open-air restaurant includes Island specialties with a Pacific Rim flair.

LOCATIONS DETAILS: Surrounded by a hotel and golf course, the activity level tends to be very lively during the day. The restaurant is open to the public for breakfast and lunch, while dinners are for private events and must be reserved in advance. Live entertainment must be preapproved by the restaurant. Dress code is casual and the venue can comfortably seat up to one hundred and fifty.

Plantation Gardens Restaurant

2253 Po'ipu Road
Koloa, Kauai, HI, 96756
877-745-2824
www.pgrestaurant.com

In a beautifully restored 1930s plantation manor house surrounded by the famous Moir Gardens, Plantation Gardens Restaurant chefs perform pure magic with their fresh fish and seafood fashioned around fresh local ingredients. All the vegetables and herbs used in the restaurant are grown organically from local farms as well as from their own garden. Kiawe, a native mesquite wood, is used on the grill, which infuses a sumptuous smoky flavor into the fish, seafood, and meats. The restaurant's wood floors, Koa furniture, and thick tropical plant life create a private romantic setting. A small lanai entrance with solid wood doors takes you into a little foyer area, where guests can gather prior to being seated. This sprawling historical marvel is the ultimate destination for an authentic Hawaiian-style reception amid towering monkey pod trees as a gentle ocean breeze nips at your earlobes.

LOCATIONS DETAILS: Specializing in private affairs and wedding receptions, this restaurant can accommodate any gathering from two people to three hundred, with professional, friendly service. Live entertainment is allowed with preapproval. The dress code is casual and it also offers off-site catering.

Roy's Poipu Bar & Grill

2360 Kiahuna Plantation Drive
Poipu, Kauai, HI 96756
808-742-5000
www.roysrestaurant.com

The extensive menu at Roy's Poipu Bar & Grill blends rich Pacific Rim cuisine with European techniques and Asian flavors, and it will have you begging for seconds. Internationally acclaimed chef Roy Yamaguchi has invented what he refers to as his "Hawaiian fusion" cuisine, which he showcases here at his Kaua'i restaurant. Roy's Poipu Bar & Grill lives up to its reputation. Offering something for nearly every taste bud, Roy's offers a lively atmosphere for the most adventurous and active couples. Privacy is not exactly an option—Roy's is a bustling place. You will come for the food at Roy's Poipu Bar & Grill, but come back for the experience.

LOCATIONS DETAILS: Located directly in the Poipu shopping center, this restaurant has an open and inviting atmosphere with low lighting and beautiful artwork on display throughout the restaurant. It can seat up to 160 people and is open nightly for dinner from 5:30 to 9:30. You can also host a fifty-person private party in the center courtyard, which has a lovely garden view (minimum $5,000 fee). The menu is known for its creative preparations and delicious desserts. Live entertainment is an option when you reserve the courtyard. Reservations are highly recommended. The dress code is casual, but no sleeveless shirts are allowed for men.

The Dining Room at The Lodge at Koele

Lobby Level, The Lodge at Koele
P.O. Box 631380
Lanai City, Lanai, HI 96763
808-565-2000 or 800-321-4666
www.fourseasons.com/koele/preview/index.html

Known for its fresh herbs, vegetables, and fruit, the formal Dining Room at The Lodge at Koele serves contemporary American cuisine featuring the freshest local seafood and Lana'i venison. Entering the main lobby you are immediately swept away by the stunning beauty of the great room. A fireplace at each end of the room is surrounded by large cozy furniture creating a warm and dreamy oasis. Guests here savor their dining experience amid a crackling fire and an impressive display of tropical orchids. Couples can then stroll along meandering pathways through ancient banyan trees while appreciating the simplicity of an elegant destination wedding and reception.

LOCATIONS DETAILS: Tucked to the back of the room, just off to the side, is the luxurious formal dining room. This restaurant can accommodate up to sixty people and is open nightly for dinner from 6 to 9:30. Reservations are required and the dress code is enforced. Collared shirts and dress slacks are required for men and resort wear is required for women.

The Terrace Restaurant at The Lodge at Koele

Lobby Level, The Lodge at Koele
P.O. Box 631380
Lanai City, Lanai, HI 96763
808-565-2000 or 800-321-4666
www.fourseasons.com/koele/preview/index.html

Overlooking the beautiful Koele Gardens, this large open-air restaurant offers classic American cuisine sustained by Hawaiian home-cooking influences. In a casual atmosphere that exudes peace and serenity, couples that dine here enjoy stunning garden views while being surrounded by a vast antique collection. The Terrace invites everyone from the hopeless romantic to the hopelessly in love.

LOCATIONS DETAILS: Parallel to the formal dining room (see page 139), the Terrace restaurant is located at the back of the great room. Group seating for up to eighty people can easily be arranged and the ambiance is cozy with low lighting and solid wood accents. Open for breakfast from 6 a. m. to 2 p.m. and dinner from 6:00 p.m. to 9:30 p.m. Reservations are recommended. The dress code is the same as the formal dining room, collared shirts and dress slacks for men, resort wear for women. No slippers are allowed. The great room, which is nearby, has live music playing from 7 to 10 nightly. Other dining options include the clubhouse at the Experience at Koele golf course, which is open for lunch till 4:30 p.m., no reservations are required.

Ihilani at Four Seasons at Manele Bay

1 Manele Bay Road
Lanai City, Lanai, HI 96763
808-565-2296
http://www.fourseasons.com/manelebay/celebrations/dining.html

For an elegant romantic dinner for two, Ihilani ("heavenly splendor") features contemporary Italian cuisine using the freshest seafood and Island-grown fruits and vegetables. Part of the Four Seasons Resort at Manele Bay, this enticing restaurant offers some of the best cuisine in Hawai'i as well as a large selection of fine wines. Exquisite décor and vast ocean views from nearly every seat in the house serve as a memorable backdrop to a delicious blend of Mediterranean and Island cuisine.

LOCATIONS DETAILS: This Italian restaurant's dark wood, maroon accents, and low lighting create a romantic atmosphere. The impeccable service will ensure a memorable evening. All seating is arranged on the outdoor terrace, and it can accommodate up to one hundred people. Open Monday through Saturday for dinner from 6 to 9:30. Live music must be preapproved by management. Reservations are recommended, and the dress code is resort wear.

Hulopo'e Court

1 Manele Bay Road
Lanai City, Lanai, HI 96763
808-565-2296
http://www.fourseasons.com/manelebay/celebrations/dining_583.html

The main dining room of the Four Seasons Lana'i was recently remodeled and renamed in honor of Hulopo'e, the pristine white-sand beach gracing the shoreline. With cuisine that reflects traditional Island favorites made with the freshest of island ingredients, Hulopo'e offers fantastic entrées that are sure to tantalize the senses. It also has a delicious gourmet breakfast buffet. Couples dining here discover traditional Island cuisine at its best. Asian accents highlight the vaulted ceiling lobby area outside both Four Seasons restaurants, where local artists display their work.

LOCATIONS DETAILS: A hostess graciously welcomes you as you arrive for dinner and escorts you to your seat. The room is open and airy, with ocean views, making it perfect for any occasion. Open for breakfast from 7 a.m. to 11 a.m. and dinner from 6 p.m. to 9:30 p.m., the main dining room area can comfortably seat 175 people. Seating arrangements include indoor/outdoor terrace dining and a separate indoor/terrace area that can be sectioned off for groups up to ninety people, which creates a more private area for your event. Other dining options include the poolside grill, which is open for lunch from 11 a.m. to 4 p.m., or you may opt for a private poolside reception. Preset menus are required for groups of twenty or more. Live music must be preapproved by management. Reservations are recommended and the dress code is casual.

RESTAURANT AND LUAU LISTINGS

Some of the top restaurants on the three islands are reviewed in the previous section of this guide, but there are many more. Here are several other fine restaurants situated near wedding ceremony venues. Luaus are another great option.

MAUI

Prince Court and Hakone
Maui Prince Resort
5400 Makena Alanui Drive
Makena, Maui, HI 96753
808-874-1111
www.princeresortshawaii.com

Banyan Tree and The Terrace
Ritz-Carlton Kapalua
1 Ritz-Carlton Drive
Kapalua, Maui, HI 96761
808-665-7211 or 800-262-8440
www.ritzcarlton.com/resorts/kapalua

Kula Lodge Restaurant
15200 Haleakala Highway
Kula, Maui, HI 96790
808-878-1535

The Maalaea Waterfront Restaurant
50 Hauoli Street
Maalaea, Maui, HI 96793
808-244-9028

Le Gunji, Restaurant Taiko, and Capische
Diamond Hawaii Resort
555 Kaukahi Street
Wailea, Maui, HI 96753
808-874-0500 or 800-800-0720
www.diamondresort.com

Sonz, Weeping Banyan, Cascades, and Spat's Trattoria
Hyatt Regency Maui
200 Nohea Kai Drive
Lahaina, Maui, HI 96761
808-667-4430 or 808-661-1234
www.maui.hyatt.com

Tropica and 'OnO Bar & Grille
Westin Maui Hotel
2365 Ka'anapali Parkway
Lahaina, Maui, HI 96761
808-661-2546 or 808-667-2525
www.westinmaui.com

Main Dining Room
Hotel Hana Maui
P.O. Box 9
Hana, Maui, HI 96713
808-248-8211 or 800-321-4262
www.hotelhanamaui.com

Hana Ranch Restaurant
5031 Hana Highway
Maui, HI 96713
808-248-8255

continued

restaurants

RESTAURANT AND LUAU LISTINGS

KAUA'I

Sushi Blues
Ching-Young Village
Shopping Center
5-5190 Kuhio Highway
Hanalei, Kauai, HI 96714
808-826-9701
www.sushiandblues.com

Tidepools and Dondero's
Grand Hyatt Kauai
1571 Po'ipu Road
Koloa, Kauai, HI 96756
808-742-1234
www.kauai.hyatt.com

Café Hanalei and La Cascata
Princeville Resort
5520 Ka Haku Road
P.O. Box 223069
Princeville, Kauai, HI 96722
800-826-4400
www.princeville.com

Shells Steak & Seafood, Amore
Naniwa, and The Point
Sheraton Kauai
2440 Hoonani Road
Koloa, Kauai, HI 96756
808-742-4037 or 808-742-1661
www.sheraton-kauai.com

Naupaka Terrace Steakhouse and
Driftwood Sandbar & Grill
Radisson Kauai Beach Resort
4331 Kaua'i Beach Drive
Lihue, Kauai, HI 96766
808-245-1955 or 800-333-3333
www.radissonkauai.com

LUAUS

Old Lahaina Lu'au
(Oceanfront, open seven days
a week)
1251 Front Street
Lahaina, Maui, HI 96761
808-667-1998
www.oldlahainaluau.com

Princeville Resort Luau
(Poolside, close to the beach;
Mondays and Thursdays)
5520 Ka Haku Road
P.O. Box 223069
Princeville, Kauai, HI 96722
800-826-4400
www.princeville.com

private properties

Hawai'i state and county laws make it nearly impossible to hold any commercial activities, such as weddings, receptions, or vacation rentals, at a private residence. The zoning alone makes it illegal. For example, if you have a property anywhere in Hawai'i that is zoned for residential, agricultural, "apartment 1, 2, 3," or anything other than commercial use, then you won't be able to rent out the location for weddings or receptions or use it as a vacation rental without applying for a special permit that takes several years and payments of tens of thousands of dollars in application fees to the county to obtain.

Private property weddings are possible only if the owners and caretakers are willing to take the risk that their neighbors or anyone else won't turn them in or file a formal complaint. If a compliant is filed, then they can be fined a thousand dollars or more per event, with more serious ramifications to follow. Now, there is what I like to refer to as "the underground": a small group of owners willing to take a risk. Often they are trying to help pay for property taxes while keeping the site undeveloped and occasionally enjoying it themselves. Some places allow you to hold your event there with a minimum seven-night stay, or they may rent it out to you by the day. However, all locations will most likely have heavy restrictions on group size, parking, choice of music and music curfews, and bathroom use. With a little research on your part via the Internet or by simply asking around, you may be able to find a property that works perfectly for you, and understanding the facts while searching will most definitely help everyone involved to achieve their dreams.

Part Three | PROFESSIONAL SERVICES

A NOTE ABOUT GRATUITY

Many of our clients ask if a gratuity is included in the prepaid wedding costs for the minister, musician, photographer, videographer, planner, and other service providers. Here in the Islands a gratuity is not included in most fees. It's never required, but if you feel that anyone has met or exceeded your expectations, a tip will be very much appreciated. Thank-you cards and letters are another way to express your appreciation and are often given with a gratuity. Mahalo!

© Mike Sydney

officiants

Religious and nonreligious ceremonies are offered by most officiants of each religion on the islands, and they are willing to perform the ceremony nearly anywhere (Catholic priests are the exception; you must be married in the church). Although a very limited number of ministers are available in each specific denomination, you may choose a nondenominational, Christian, Hawaiian-style, or Jewish wedding ceremony, a commitment ceremony, or a civil ceremony conducted by a justice of the peace. You must obtain a marriage license application prior to the wedding and bring it with you so that your minister (and witnesses if you so choose) can sign it. Your minister will then send in the completed license application to the Department of Health, which will take four to five months to issue you an official copy of your license. It is illegal for your minister to make a copy of this application to give to you for any reason. When you apply for your license, your agent will provide a form for you to send in with a fee if you would like to expedite this process.

Minister's fees range from $100 to $750 and can double on holidays or remote location venues. Ministers have different requirements, so be sure to ask whether they prefer meeting you prior to the wedding day, whether you can change the standard ceremony features, and what they wear as their preferred formal attire for the ceremony. Most officiants will offer a Hawaiian lei exchange as part of the ceremony. This tradition involves the bride and groom presenting each other with a special lei followed by a kiss on the cheek.

It is also possible to bring your own minister from home, and the process is an easy one as long as he or she is a licensed minister. A simple application can be obtained from the state Department of Health (at www.hawaii.gov/doh), which will issue your minister a one-day license for the state of Hawai'i. If you want to bring someone to perform the ceremony who is not licensed, then you have to hire a licensed officiant from the state of Hawai'i to co-officiate by pronouncing you husband and wife, signing the marriage license application, and sending it in.

OFFICIANTS

MAUI

Traditional

David Kreuger
2218 Auina Place
Kihei, HI 96753
808-879-7979

Robert McCollor
P.O. Box 1267
Kihei, HI 96753
808-242-5959

Ron Winckler
P.O. Box 1657
Kihei, HI 96753
808-874-9899

Hawaiian Style

Laki Kaahumanu
168 Prison Street
Lahaina, HI 96761
808-667-0423

Jessie Nakooka
P.O. Box 37
Makawao, HI 96768
808-572-7290
nakooka@gte.net

Tino Rosete
P.O. Box 88072
Pukulani, HI 96788
808-572-0995

Vance Rosete
461 South Lono Avenue
Kahului, HI 96732
808-280-9013
info@pastorvance.com

Paul Tangonan
142 Baker Street
Lahaina, HI 96761
808-661-0420

Alapaki "Al" Terry
194 Kamakoi Loop
Kihei, HI 96753
808-879-7149
alapaki@maui.net

Jewish

Robert Gillman
P.O. Box 733
Kihei, HI 96753
808-879-9932

Rabbi David Glickman
634 Alulike Street
Kihei, HI 96753
808-874-5397

Joseph Narrowe
17 Pahee Place
Kahului, HI 96732
808-572-0515

Rose Roslinsky
154 Auoli Drive
Makawao, HI 96768
808-572-2141   **continued**

officiants

OFFICIANTS

Justices of the Peace

Judge Joseph Cardosa
2145 Main Street
Wailuku, HI 96793
808-244-2929

Judge Rhonda Loo
1085 Kuhio Place
Wailuku, HI 96793
808-244-2727,
808-357-1691 (cell)

Judge Boyd Mossman
121 Ala Apapa Place
Makawao, HI 96768
808-572-9192

KAUA'I

M. Leilani K. Kaleiohi, Kahu
P.O. Box 736
Kilauea, HI 96754
808-821-0453
mlkk@aloha.net

Rev. Caroline C. Miura, Kahu
5060-A Kawaihau Road
Kapaa, HI 96746
808-652-4432
therev@gte.net

Jeane Michioka
hulagirl1818@hotmail.com

Claire Vierkoetter
P.O. Box 223185
Princeville, HI 96722
808-826-9737
b.kw@verizon.net

Manulele and Bridget Clarke
P.O. Box 445
Anahola, HI 96703
808-821-1698
manulele@hawaiilink.net

Larry A. LaSota
5345 Hoonoiki Road
Princeville, HI 96722
866-481-8825 or 808-826-0044

LANA'I

Michael Gannon
P.O. Box 630413
Lanai City, HI 96763
808-559-9600

Beverly Zigmond
P.O. Box 631067
Lanai City, HI 96763
808-565-6633
bzigmond@bigfoot.com

Pastor Nohea Kuhai
Church of God
P.O. Box 631175
Lanai City, HI 96763
808-559-0692

caterers

Whatever it takes to make your day special, a reputable caterer along with their expert staff can create a menu that your guests will not soon forget. Catering companies are only necessary for your cocktail reception or dinner when your venue is at a private property. Some caterers will suggest sample menus; others prefer that you give them an idea of the meal you would like to be served so that they can put together a quote for a menu based on your requests. Any caterer can also make suggestions as to the preparation for each course. For the main course, for example, you could decide on chicken, fish, lobster, steak, or prime rib, and then allow the caterer to suggest a preparation. Similarly, you can request certain side dishes or ask the caterer to make suggestions. At a private venue you will need to rent tables, linens, chairs, plateware, stemware, and all the other necessary accoutrements. Some caterers have the ability to provide these items, and some do not. Sit-down dinners are much harder to carry off at a private property because most properties have limited kitchen facilities. Most caterers have a liquor license for off-site events and they can supply a bartender and the condiments, or you can opt to provide alcoholic beverages on your own.

If you are getting married at a resort, your wedding cakes must be prepared by its pastry chef to conform to state of Hawai'i health codes. Resorts will make a standard-design wedding cake. Special requests have to be made in advance by providing a photo for a custom quote. Cake tastings are extremely hard to do unless you have the budget to fly out months in advance (and additional fees will apply). Outside the resort venue, many independent pastry chefs can make you a wedding cake and even deliver it for a small fee. Restaurants will allow you to bring in a wedding cake from an outside source, although cake-cutting fees may apply.

CATERERS

MAUI

Ritz-Carlton Kapalua
1 Ritz-Carlton Drive
Kapalua, HI 86761
808-669-6200
www.mauiritz.com

Celebrations
900 Hali'imaile Road
Hailiimaile, HI 96768
808-572-4946
www.bevgannonrestaurants.com

Four Seasons Resort
3900 Wailea Alanui Drive
Wailea, HI 96753
808-874-8000
www.fourseasons.com/maui

KAUA'I

Contemporary Flavors
1610 Haleukani Street
Lihue, HI 96766
808-245-2522

Blossoming Lotus (vegan)
1384 Kuhio Highway
Kapaa, HI 96746
808-823-6658
gia@blossominglotus.com

Heavenly Creations on the Beach
P.O. Box 167
Anahola, HI 96703
877-828-1700
www.heavenlycreations.org
info@heavenlycreations.org

Tropical Chefs
5820 Meli Place
Kapaa, HI 96746
808-651-7146
www.tropicaldinner.com
tropicaldinner@hawaiian.net

Wedding Cakes

Stillwells Bakery
1740 Kaahumanu Avenue
Wailuku, Maui, HI 96793
808-243-2243

Cakewalk Paia Bakery
P.O. Box 790196
Paia, Maui, HI 96779
808-579-8770
www.cakewalkmaui.com

photographers and videographers

Not all photography and videography services are created equal. Here in the Islands the general rule is that the pricing is proportionate to the creativity and experience of the practitioner. Only a handful of photographers and an even smaller number of videographers are highly skilled, so booking early is important in securing the best. It is essential to see the work of the person you are considering. If you are coordinating your own wedding, then I would suggest that you interview photographers to see if their style is in line with your expectations. There are traditional-style, photojournalistic, candid, and cutting-edge "avant-garde" portraiture styles to consider, so knowing which style you prefer will save you hours of time when selecting your vendor(s). Be careful when selecting your videography service. Many companies offer "home video style" at a reasonable cost, but only a few can deliver a professionally produced wedding movie.

Most video packages include two hours of "coverage" time, which means the videographer will be with you for that amount of time, not shoot every second of that time. Movie packages often include exclusive Hawaii scenery, pre-wedding activity, and professional editing that can include black-and-white, slow-motion, and special effects, as well as a personalized music overlay, titling, and a keepsake video or DVD album. Prices range from $400 to $1,500 for the most basic package. Most basic photography packages also include two hours of coverage time and twenty-four photographs in a standard album. For photography, prices also range from $400 to $900 for the smallest package. Negatives of your photos or raw copies of your video are not always included as part of the service. Most professionals discourage or do not allow other professional photographers and videographers to shoot over their shoulders during your event.

Please provide a break and meal for your photographer, videographer, and assistants, especially when selecting a package that is four hours or more. Everyone needs to get a glass of water, eat, and go to the restroom, so be respectful of your help.

Finally, remember that this is your special day. Photographers and videographers should be there to capture the moment, not create it. It is important to be at ease. Standing on the other side of a camera is not something you usually do for hours at a time. If you're not comfortable, you may feel and see your anxiety in the final photos and video. So, relax, smile and live in the moment with the love of your life beside you as professionals capture one of the most significant events of your life.

PHOTOGRAPHERS AND VIDEOGRAPHERS

MAUI

A & C Photography
P.O. Box 298
Kihei, HI 96753
808-875-1100
www.photosbymichael.com

John Henry Photography
59A Kanoa Street
Wailuku, HI 96793
808-242-1918
jhphoto@hawaii.rr.com
www.johnhenryphotography.com

La ano Photography by
Graham Chappell
808-870-6399
graham@laano.com
www.laano.com

Photography by Bill Stockwell
3365 Akala Drive
Kihei, HI 96753
808-879-7200
www.mauiweddingphotographer.com

MauiFoto Photography
Daniel Sullivan and Carla Jalbert
939 Lower Hogback Road
Haiku, HI 96708
808-575-2838
daniel@mauifoto.com
www.mauifoto.com

Mike Sydney
1 Main Plaza
200 Main Street, Suite 540
Wailuku, HI 96793
888-505-2808 or 808-249-2808
mike@mikesidneyphotographer.com
www.mikesidneyphotographer.com

Peter Thompson
P.O. Box 959, Number 301
Kihei, HI 96753
808-891-2015
www.photohawaii.com

Hawaii Video Memories
230 Hana Highway, Suite 11
Kahului, HI 96732
808-871-5788
www.hawaiivideomemories.com

Surefire Productions
332 Wainohia Streeet
Kihei, HI 96753
808-874-8230
mike@surefireproductions.com
www.surefireproductions.com

Island Production Group
Todd Mizomi
P.O. Box 434
Kahului, Maui, HI 96732
808-281-5755

continued

photographers and videographers

PHOTOGRAPHERS AND VIDEOGRAPHERS

KAUA'I

Nick Galante Photography
4235 Pu'u Pinao Place
Koloa, HI 96756
888-742-8372 or 808-742-8372
nick@kauaiphoto.com
www.kauaiphoto.com

Kilohana Photography
(Stephen Gnazzo)
P.O. Box 110
Lawai, Kauai, HI 96765
808-332-9637
808-332-9588
kp@eventphotos4u.com
http://youreventimages.com

Photo-Spectrum
2987 Umi Street
Lihue, HI 96766
808-245-7667
www.photo-spectrum.com

Profile Productions
P.O. Box 222038
Princeville, HI 96722
808-826-0044
info@kauaiweddingvideos.com
www.kauaiweddingvideos.com

Rainbow Photography
(Blaine and Jeane Michioka)
P.O. Box 1143
Kapaa, HI 96746
888-828-0555 or 808-828-0555
rainbow@aloha.net
www.rainbowphoto.com

Dianne Reynolds Photography
P.O. Box 385
Hanalei, HI 96714
888-828-4877
dianne@photophotokauai.com
www.photophotokauai.com

Studio Gelston Dwight
P.O. Box 1065
Lihue, HI 96766
808-822-3686
g@gelson.com
www.gelston.com

Video Lynx
(Bob and Darla Cox)
276 Aina Pua Place
Kapaa, HI 96746
808-821-1367
sales@videolynxkauai.com
www.videolynxkauai.com

Frances Woods Photography
P.O. Box 1158
Hanalei, HI 96714
808-828-2177
f.woods2@verizon.net
www.kauai-photographer.com

**PHOTOGRAPHERS AND
VIDEOGRAPHERS**

LANA'I

Jeffrey Asher Digital Imaging Systems
808-565-2200 or 808-559-0122
ash-inc@aloha.net
www.lanaiweddings.com

Joe West Photography
P.O. Box 631172
Lanai City, HI 96763
808-565-6219
joelanai@yahoo.com
www.joewestphoto.com

musicians and entertainers

There is nothing like live music to set the mood and add a special element to the ambience of your wedding day. A recording just doesn't do the occasion justice. Besides, you can hear prerecorded music anytime you want. Live music makes your wedding much more personalized. There are many styles to choose from, and for a nominal fee and with a little advance notice, nearly every musician can learn a specific song that may not already be in their repertoire. Sample CDs are not typically available, so a wedding coordinator familiar with the quality of music is helpful when you are selecting the perfect performer.

Some possibilities: acoustical guitarist-singer, classical guitarist (no vocals), Hawaiian slack-key guitarist (no vocals), ukulele player, keyboard/organist, flutist, cellist, and violinist. The guitar will truly incorporate Hawai'i's culture into the occasion or to add a fuller and more realistic sound, you can select two instruments to create a duo or trio of your own. If you're not familiar with the traditional music of the Islands, you can allow your musician(s) the freedom to choose appropriate Hawaiian-style music for your special day, which I find is what most couples seem to prefer.

If you are at a location where you need to amplify your ceremony (near ocean or waterfall), then you also should look into renting battery-powered amplification. (Note: Most musicians are very conscientious about their instruments. They will prefer to be located in the shade and will run for cover if it starts to sprinkle.) The price of most musicians ranges from $125 to $300 per hour. Custom quotes are given if a second location is requested or if you would like them to continue at your cocktail or reception venue. In addition to musicians, you can engage the services of Hawaiian entertainers such as Polynesian drummers, conch shell blowers, torch maiden escorts, and ceremonial dance performers. These and your duos, trios, and bands can give you custom quotes based on your specific requests. DJs are also an option in selected locations. Prices for any of those options range from $150 to $400 per vendor per hour. Many locations have music restrictions as well as music curfews, so please check with your wedding coordinator or selected wedding venue for further information.

MUSICIANS AND ENTERTAINERS

MAUI

Guitar

Tom Conway
100 Waipalani Road
Haiku, HI 96708
808-572-2078
tomconway@hawaii.rr.com

Vance Koenig
P.O. Box 876
Kula, HI 96790
808-573-3935
rosewood@maui.net

Jamie Lawrence
P.O. Box 127
Kahului, HI 96733
808-875-6700
bookjamie@mac.com

Tim Ohara
50 Poha Place
Pukalani, HI 96768
808-572-1272
options@maui.net

Stephanie R. A. Pszyk
1270-A Haiku Road
Haiku, HI 96708
808-575-9573
snap@mac.com

Hale Villiarmo
P.O. Box 591
Kahului, HI 96733
808-281-4913
hale@maui.net

Harp

Heavenly Harps of Hawaii
Celia Canty
P.O. Box 1571
Kihei, HI 96753
808-874-3836
harpinfo@heavenlyharps.com

Maui Harps
(Kristine Snyder)
1046 Kupulau Drive
Kihei, HI 96753
808-891-0061
dandk@mauiharps.com

Ginny Morgan
745 Mililani Place
Kihei, Maui, HI 96753
808-879-4453
gmorgan@maui.net

Elaine Olson
(Weekends only)
17 Upu Place
Kula, HI 96790
808-878-6958

continued

musicians and entertainers

MUSICIANS AND ENTERTAINERS

Maria Valentine
P.O. Box 1102
Makawao, HI 96768
808-572-6796
mariavalentine@verizon.net

Cello

Mioko Grine
715 South Kihei Road, Apt. 202
Kihei, HI 96753
808-876-1116 or
920-231-0176 (Summers only)

Ginny Morgan
745 Mililani Place
Kihei, HI 96753
808-879-4453
gmorgan@maui.net

Michelle Romero
60 Kunihi Lane
Kahului, HI 96732
808-893-0187

Keyboards

Danny Brown
P.O. Box 976
Kihei, HI 96753
808-875-0854
dannyb@maui.net

Pam Petersen
893 Olena Street
Wailuku, HI 96793
808-243-2265
pampetersen@netscape.net

Violin

Richard Cook
P.O. Box 1027
Haiku, HI 96708
808-575-9724
rbcman@hotmail.com
also plays viola

Joan Hayden
71A Ulana Street
Makawao, HI 96768
808-573-5325

Don Lax
P.O. Box 959
Kihei, HI 96753
808-283-6942 (cell)
donvlax@maui.net

Roland NoNo
929 East Onaha Place
Wailuku, HI 96793
808-242-7112

Willie Wainright
16 Kekaulike Avenue
Kula, HI 96790
808-372-4053
willie@country-music.ch

MUSICIANS AND ENTERTAINERS

Flute

Ann Durham
129 Lopaka Place
Kula, HI 96790
808-250-6920 (cell)

Flute Music Maui
Barry Pono Fried
P.O. Box 324
Makawao, HI 96768
808-572-3483
openeye@aloha.net

Jean Pierre Thoma
49 Lopaka Place
Kula, HI 96790
808-870-5533

Saxophone

David Choy
830 Hoomau Street
Wailuku, HI 96793
808-276-7884

Jean Pierre Thoma
49 Lopaka Place
Kula, HI 96790
808-870-5533

Hawaiian Entertainment, Bands, and DJs

Cool Steel
P.O. Box 1796
Makawao, HI 96768
808-572-4755

Kelly Covington
231 A Waipahe Place
Kihei, Maui, HI 96753
808-879-1871
kjazz56@aol.com

CVP Entertainment, Inc.
P.O. Box 827
Kihei, HI 96753-0827
808-875-4450
cvpentertainment@juno.com

Envisions Entertainment
381 Huku Li'i Place, Suite 3
Kihei, HI 96753
808-874-1000
www.envisionsentertainment.com

Jimmy Mac and the Cool Cats
P.O. Box 750
Kula, HI 96790
808-572-1258

Maui Tunes (DJ services)
P.O. Box 1654
Kihei, HI 96753
808-276-6036
www.mauitunes.com

continued

musicians and entertainers

MUSICIANS AND ENTERTAINERS

Musical Options
50 Poha Place
Pukalani, HI 96768
808-572-1271
options@maui.net

Tihati Productions
360 Ho'ohana Street, Suite 208
Kahului, HI 96732
808-877-7627
theresa@tihati.com

Dan Viola
(DJ services)
1895 Ka'ahele Place
Kihei, HI 96753
808-283-0124
dviola1234@aol.com

KAUA'I

Rick Avalon
(Keyboards and vocals)
P.O. Box 1436
Kiluea, HI 96754
808-828-0463

Manulele Clarke
(Ukulele and vocals)
P.O. Box 445
Anahola, HI 96703
808-821-1698 or
808-652-2995 (cell)
Pat Cockett

(Slack-key guitar, ukulele,
songwriting)
4558 Ekolu Street
Lihue, HI 96766
808-245-5792 or 808-651-1274

Carmen Dragon
(Harp)
P.O. Box 1302
Kiluea, HI 96754
808-826-0063

Celestial Music
P.O. Box 1302
Kilauea, HI 96754
808-826-0346 or 877-823-5378
www.celestialmusicartists.com
carmen@midpac.net

Ken Emmerson
(Guitar)
808-828-6862

Lady Ipo Kahaunaele
(Ukulele, vocals, emceeing)
P.O. Box 129
Anahola, HI 96703
808-652-5485 or 808-821-8876

Kirby Keough
(Guitar and vocals)
4160 Hoala, Suite #9H
Lihue, HI 99766
808-651-4597
keoughkoo1@hawaii.rr.com

MUSICIANS AND ENTERTAINERS

Anela Lauren
(Harpists for all occasions)
P.O. Box 1242
Kapaa, HI 96746
808-639-4356
www.anela.byregion.net

Gordon Marron
(Violin and keyboards)
P.O. Box 1888
Koloa, HI 96756
808-742-1090
gordon@kauaimusicalarts.com

Hal Kinnaman
(Guitar)
P.O. Box 118
Hanapepe, HI 96716
808-335-0322
www.halkinnaman.com

Paul Togioka
(Guitar)
808-823-8822,
808-241-5054 (pager)
www.paultogioka.com

Pancho Graham
(Guitar, ukulele, violin)
P.O. Box 427
Kilauea, HI 96754
808-828-1252
panchhog@hotmail.com

Norman Ka'awa Soloman
(Guitar, vocals)
P.O. Box 669
Anahola, HI 96703
808-651-8386
kaawa_music@hotmail.com

Kustom Sounds Kauai
DJ Michael Dandurand
P.O. Box 662344
Puhi, HI 96766
808-245-7860
ksk@hawaii.rr.com
www.kskauai.com

LANA'I

LD Productions
P.O. Box 630486
Lanai City, HI 96763
808-565-6955
dje@aloha.net
www.ldproductions.com

Rabaca Drive Entertainment
P.O. Box 630304
Lanai City, HI 96763
808-565-6670
rabaca@aloha.net

florists

There are many floral details to think about for your wedding day. Arrangements for leis, custom ribbons and greenery, floral pathways, arches, chairs, the chapel, the reception hall, and centerpieces are a few. Fresh flowers for your cake that match your other wedding flowers are also a nice detail. Looking through magazines and roaming the Web will give you a head start in deciding what you want.

Believe it or not, it is often extremely difficult to obtain specific flowers that you may see in magazines or on the Web. Commercial growers are not as abundant on the Islands as many people think, and there simply aren't enough islands to grow all the flowers needed to meet the demand. A very large percentage of flowers are shipped in from other islands as well as other countries, making flower arrangements more expensive than anywhere else in America. The best tropical flowers flourish in Hawai'i, but they are very heavy and very large, not really appropriate wedding flowers.

Therefore, I suggest choosing your color scheme first, before you select the specific flowers. Standard flowers like a rose can easily be obtained as long as they're in season. Custom flowers such as lilies of the valley, Black Magic roses, and sweet peas are more challenging for florists to obtain and are often ordered from abroad at an additional expense— and even then there is no guarantee you'll get them. If a crop in Holland fails, then you will most likely have to select another flower at the last minute. It helps to find out what's easily available on the island during the time of year you're planning to wed. Ask your wedding coordinator or florist of choice for suggestions of specific flowers that are in line with your color scheme.

Floral enhancements can take over your budget if you let them, so unless you have an unlimited flower budget it helps to be flexible. You'll have many styles of bouquets to choose from: cascading, hand-tied/French, and nosegay are a few. On average, bouquets range from $100 to $500 (depending on the quality, your flower selections, the size, and style). In addition, the florists who pay more attention to detail and offer the freshest flowers will be the most expensive.

On the other hand, you should not skimp on your flowers, either. Flowers are one of the most important enhancements of a wedding, and your investment will bring you joy on your wedding day as well as in the future when you look at your photos or video. Doing your flowers on your own or trying to create arrangements after your arrival is not recommended because of the time involved, the unpredictable availability of flowers, and the last-minute stress.

florists

FLORISTS

MAUI

Asa Flowers
1063 Main Street, Suite C-202
Wailuku, HI 96793
808-249-8845

Country Bouquets
1043 Makawao Avenue
Makawao, HI 96768
808-572-6928

Anny Heid Flowers, LLC
P.O. Box 1890
Makawao, HI 96768
808-572-7033
anny@annyheidflowers.com
www.annyheidflowers.com

Napili Florist
Napili Plaza
1595 Napilihau Street
Kapalua, HI 96761
808-669-4861
stanfields@verizon.net

KAUA'I

Mr. Flowers
P.O. Box 223300
Princeville, HI 96722
888-828-6641
kokea@hawaiian.net

The Blue Orchid
5470 Koloa Road
Koloa, HI 96756
808-742-9094
info@blueorchidkauai.com
www.blueorchidkauai.com

Florescence Kauai
2488-D Kaumualii Highway
Kalaheo, HI 96741
808-332-7673
florescence@kauaiflorist.com
www.kauaiflorist.com

Tammy's Flowers and Gifts
P.O. Box 510118
Kealia, HI 96751
808-822-1844
piilani1@hawaii.rr.com

LANA'I

For your wedding on this island, all of your flower arrangements have to be brought in from Maui. You will need to set aside twice as much for your florals in your overall wedding budget.

beauty services and spa treatments

Meticulous preparation goes into looking good on your wedding day. Your hair, skin, nails, and overall spiritual well-being are important for that newlywed glow. A spa treatment is a wonderful way to relax and rejuvenate. Resorts offer a private, serene location for a bride and her wedding party. Smaller individual spas not located at a resort offer a quainter environment. There are also cosmetologists that go on location. Just keep in mind that it takes about an hour and a half to do hair and makeup combined for one person. This means if you have three bridesmaids and only one cosmetologist you will have to get an early start. The benefit is that you don't have to leave your room. Prices range from $150 to$225 for hair and makeup per person. You may pay a little bit more for in-room service if you have bridesmaids, but many brides feel that the convenience is well worth the expense. Salons know their schedules three months in advance and discourage booking prior to that. Phone consultations are usually done at no charge. It is helpful to bring a picture of the style you are interested in, but if you are still nervous, then you may do a trial run at the same cost. Also it's best to get your manicures and pedicures done prior to the day of the ceremony. That way there will be plenty of time for your nails to dry fully prior to using them for the many tasks required in getting ready.

BEAUTY AND SPA

MAUI

Maui Day Spa
808-879-0437
www.mauidayspa.com

Spa Grande at the Grand
Wailea Resort
3850 Wailea Alanui Drive
Wailea, HI 96753
800-888-6100
www.grandwailea.com

Four Seasons Resort and
Orchid Salon
3900 Wailea Alanui
Wailea, HI 96753
808-874-8000
www.fourseasons.com/maui

Fairmont's Salon and Spa
Juvenal & Co. Hair Salon
Spa Kealani
4100 Wailea Alanui
Wailea, HI 96753
808-879-4247 or 808-874-4100
juvenal@hawaii.rr.com

Honua Spa at the Hotel
Hana Maui
P.O. Box 9
Hana, HI 96713
808-270-5290 ext. 5290
spa@hotelhanamaui.com

Spa Moana at the Hyatt
Regency Maui Resort
200 Nohea Kai Drive
Lahaina, HI 96761
808-661-1234
www.maui.hyatt.com

The Spa at the Westin Maui
2365 Ka'anapali Parkway
Kaanapali, HI 96761
808-661-2588
www.westinmaui.com

KAUA'I

Anara Spa at the Hyatt
Regency Kauai
1571 Po'ipu Road
Koloa, HI 96756
808-742-1234
www.anaraspa.com

LANA'I

Four Seasons Lana'i and Spa
1 Manele Bay Road
Lanai City, HI 96763
808-565-2000
www.fourseasons.com/
manelebay

continued

beauty services and spa treatments

BEAUTY AND SPA

In-Room Hair and Makeup (Maui only)

Robbie Marochi
808-879-0437
www.mauidayspa.com

Jean Muldoon
155 Wailea Ike Place
Number 96
Kihei, HI 96753
808-870-9087
jeanmm@hawaii.rr.com

Tanya Peterson
30 Waima Haihaig Street
Kihei, HI 96753
808-281-1188
www.ultimatehawaii.com/tanya

Joan Davenport
1656 Ku'uipo Street
Lahaina, HI 96761
808-661-1690
www.adesignofbeauty.com

© Bill Stockwell

rental companies

There are a limited amount of rental companies capable of meeting all your wedding needs. Some companies rent only chairs, linens, plate-ware, stem-ware, and silverware and other items for a reception dinner at a private location. Other rental companies provide stages, dance floors, back-drops, arches, lighting, plants, and other items for a themed event. If you're lucky, one rental company will be able to provide you with all that you're looking for. Ask to see photos from the company so you know exactly what you're getting. Find out if setup, delivery, and removal are included in your quote. Some companies will simply drop off your items, and you will have to put one of your family members or guests to work to get things set up. Rental companies are very selective in their drop-off locations, and some of them have minimum fees. Drop-off and pickup times are an issue at certain locations, so make sure you get all the details prior to making a commitment. Refunds are not given in case you have to cancel for inclement weather.

You may want to consider renting a tent for some outdoor reception locations. Prices are typically $500 to $4,500, which includes setup, delivery, and removal. Only certain types of arches will work on the beach, while other types of arches are better for private properties or cliffside locations, so be specific with your vendor. Floral décor for your arch can dramatically increase the expense. Some florists can also provide you with certain rental items (arches, centerpiece containers, custom linens, high-end chairs, and so on) so you will need to explore all your options if you plan on doing this on your own.

RENTAL COMPANIES

MAUI

Event Designers International
2715 Kauhale Street
Kihei, HI 96753
808-875-6030
www.hulaexpress.com

Envisions Entertainment
381 Huku Li'i Place, Suite 3
Kihei, HI 96753
808-874-1000
www.envisionsentertainment.com

Maui Rents
296 Alamaha Street
Number Z-3
Kahului, HI 96732
808-877-5827

KAUA'I

Kauai Tent and Party Rental
Chris Carswell
P.O. Box 963
Kilauea, Kauai, HI 96754
808-828-1597
www.kauaitent.com

LANA'I

Any rental items not available through the resorts will have to be brought in from Maui, adding an additional expense to your overall budget.

© Mike Sydney

Part Four | TRAVEL AND ACCOMMODATIONS

travel agents

I highly recommend that you enlist the help of a reputable travel agent to help you organize all your travel. An agent can constantly search for the lowest airfare, present you with economical air, car, and accommodation packages, and discuss all the options available to you and your guests. The following travel agents have helped many of my clients secure their air reservations and accommodations. These agents are experienced in travel to Hawai'i, and they offer personalized service and expertise.

Island Style Travel
Kim Jenkins
P.O. Box 1078
Makawao, Maui, HI 96768
808-572-6995

Hawaiian Island Vacations
(Land reservations only)
415-A Dairy Road
Kahului, Maui, HI 96732
808-871-4981
www.hawaiianisland.com/travel
travel@hawaiianisland.com

airline information

United and Delta are the main carriers of choice when flying nonstop from the West Coast directly to Hawai'i. The flight takes approximately five hours. Other airlines that serve the islands include American, Aloha Airlines, and Hawaiian Airlines.

I recommend that you either ship your wedding dress in advance or take it aboard the plane as one of your carry-on items. In my experience most of the airlines are very nice about helping you find an appropriate space to store your wedding dress during the flight. Over the years, I have had several clients lose their luggage to the airlines' dysfunctional baggage systems yet have never lost a wedding gown through FedEx, UPS, or Express Mail.

Once you arrive and pick up your car, you should plan on driving at least thirty minutes in any direction to reach your hotel. If you don't have a map of the island, don't worry. Every airport has free maps.

FOR DOMESTIC TRAVEL

American Airlines
www.aa.com
800-433-7300

Delta Air Lines
www.delta.com
800-221-1212

United Airlines
www.united.com
800-864-8331

Aloha Airlines
www.alohaairlines.com
800-367-5250

Hawaiian Airlines
www.hawaiianair.com
800-367-5320

AIRPORT CODES

MAUI
- Kahului Airport (OGG) is the main public terminal.
- Kapalua Airport (JHM) accommodates smaller aircraft.
- Hana Airport (HNM) allows only private aircraft.

KAUA'I
- Lihu'e Airport (LIH) is the only public airport.
- Port Allen Airport (PAK) accommodates smaller aircraft.

LANA'I
- Lana'i Airport (LNY) is the only public airport.

accommodations

Where to stay is always a big question. Do you want to be fully pampered? What kind of budget do you have? Do you want to eat out all the time? Do you want to feel as though you are on vacation? Those are all important questions that you, your family, and your friends need to ask before deciding on what type of accommodations to start looking into. You can stay at a lavish resort, a condo, a B&B, or even a private home. Condos are a nice compromise: most of them are on the beach, with pools, a kitchen (so that you don't have to eat out all the time), lanais, barbecue areas with pavilions, and large outdoor grassy areas. You don't have to stay at a resort to get married there, and you can stay at one resort while marrying at another, so you are virtually unrestricted when it comes to your accommodations. The cost of renting a private home can be comparable to that of staying at a resort, but it will give you much more privacy along with the ability to blend in with the community. This ultimately makes it feel like a home away from home. Another popular option is for the bride and groom to stay at a resort while family and friends stay at condos. This way you and your guests can all utilize the resort facilities, yet spend less money overall.

In general, a standard room at a beachfront resort will cost upwards of $350 a night, and you will have to eat out for every meal. Condos cost $200 and more a night, while private residences can range from $300 to thousands a night, depending on how elaborate a location you want. (Note that there is some controversy over the legality of B&B properties and private homes.) Following are a few of the many condos available. These offer you the best amenities, well-kept and contemporary units, while offering a good location on the island.

ACCOMMODATIONS

MAUI

Kaanapali Alii
($360–$600)
50 Nohea Kai Drive
Lahaina, Maui, HI 96761
800-642-6284 or 808-667-1400
www.kaanapalialii.com

Kahana Village
($150–$400)
4531 Lower Honoapi'ilani Road
Lahaina, Maui, HI 96761
800-824-3065 or 808-669-5111
www.kahanavillage.com

Mahina Surf
($185–$350)
4057 Lower Honoapi'ilani Road
Lahaina, Maui, HI 96761
800-367-6086 or 808-669-6068
www.mahina-surf.com

Destination Resorts
($185–$880)
Six resorts in south Maui: Ekahi,
Ekolu, Elua, Makena Surf, Polo Beach,
Grand Champions
808-891-6200 or 800-367-5246
infor@drhmaui.com
www.drhmaui.com

Kamaole Sands
($195–$485)
2695 South Kihei Road
Kihei, Maui, HI
800-367-5004, or 808-874-8700
www.castleresorts.com/KSM

KAUA'I

Embassy Vacation Po'ipu Point
($295–$1,000)
1613 Pe'e Road
Koloa, Kauai, HI 96756
808-742-1888 or 800-426-3350
www.marcresorts.com
www.kauaiembassy.com/

Outrigger at Lae Nani Resort
The Coconut Coast
($240–$355)
410 Papaloa Road
Kapaa, Kauai, HI 96746
808-822-4938 or 800-688-7444
www.outrigger.com
$240–$355

Hanalei Colony Resort
($180–$335)
5380 Honoiki Road
Princeville, Kauai, HI 96722
808-826-6522 or 877-997-6667
www.hanalei-bay-resort.com

continued

accommodations

ACCOMMODATIONS

Kauai Regency Resort
Condominiums
($225–$600)
2381 Hoohu Road
Koloa, Kauai, HI 96756
866-695-2824
www.kauairegency.com

Lanikai Resort
($275–$385)
390 Papaloa Road
Kapaa, Kauai, HI 96746
808-822-7700 or 800-755-2824
www.castleresorts.com

LANA'I

Hotel Lana'i
($95–$135)
828 Lana'i Avenue
Lanai City, Lanai, HI 96763
808-565-7211 or 800-795-7211
808-565-6450 (fax)
www.hotellanai.com

The Fairway Terraces at Manele
($400–$5,000)
P.O. Box 630310
Lanai City, Lanai, HI 96763
808-565-4800 or 800-505-2624
www.lanailuxuryhomes.com/
manele/fairwayterraces

transportation

While you're visiting, you'll discover that bus and other public transportation on the Islands is generally very limited. Most resorts offer a free shuttle service to and from popular areas like shopping centers. Taxis are available by calling in advance.

Nonetheless, you can easily arrive at your wedding ceremony in style. Transportation services on the Islands cater to both the romantic and the adventurous. You can choose to arrive by classic car, limousine, town car, horse and carriage, taxi, motorcycle, helicopter, limo SUV, limo bus, and—let's not forget—canoe. Red-carpet service is standard procedure for reputable limousine companies, and they decorate the car for after the ceremony. Expect to pay $100 to $300 per hour. Some limo companies charge a two-hour minimum, and your time begins at their home base, so get a quote from the company or your wedding coordinator prior to securing your transportation. If your destination is only fifteen minutes away, you may want to use a standard rental vehicle to save on costs. Work with your travel agent to get the best deals on rental cars for you and your guests.

TRANSPORTATION

MAUI

Wailea Limousine Service
P.O. Box 428
Wailuku, Maui, HI 96793
808-875-4114
www.wailealimo.com

Akina Aloha Tours
(Limo buses, horse and carriage,
classic cars)
P.O. Box 933
Kihei, Maui, HI 96753
808-879-2828
www.akinatours.com

The Limo Company
(Sedans and Lincoln Navigators)
P.O. Box 959 PMB 530
Kihei, Maui, HI 96753
808-357-0936 or 808-891-0200

Arthur's Limousine
283 Lalo Street, Suite H
Kahului, Maui, HI 96732
808-871-5555
www.arthurslimo.com

continued

transportation

TRANSPORTATION

KAUA'I

Kauai North Shore Limousine
and Tours
P.O. Box 109
Kilauea, Kauai, HI 96754
808-634-7260
northshorelimo@verizon.net
www.kauainorthshorelimo.com

Plantation Carriages
3-2243 Kaumuali'i Highway
Lihue, Kauai, HI 96766
808-246-9529 or 877-877-8908
pcarriage@hawaiian.net
www.theweddingcarriage.com

LANA'I

Rabaca's Limousine and Tour Co.
P.O. Box 630304
Lanai City, Lanai, HI 96763
808-565-6670
rabaca@aloha.net

© Michael Andrews

Part Five | DESTINATION PLANNER

first steps

Planning plays an important role in the success of your special day. You should start the wedding preparations at least six months in advance (and most often before then to secure your airfare and accommodations). This will allow you a larger selection of services when seeking out the very best that the Islands have to offer. The top people are always booked well in advance, and since availability is on a first-come, first-served basis, other couples, convention groups, sports groups, and local events are competing to secure high-quality services, breathtaking locations, and luxurious accommodations at the same time.

Open communication with your fiancé is the most important first step you can take. To set the foundation, write down what you both want, determine the size of the wedding, assemble a guest list, discuss your ideal location, and draft a preliminary budget. During the process it's important to be thoughtful of each other's wishes, to be flexible while keeping a sense of humor, and to spend time enjoying each other so that you never lose sight of what brought you together. Any dilemmas you then face will be minor compared to the love that you have for each other.

A SPECIAL NOTE ABOUT FAMILY AND FRIENDS

Because of all of the coordination needed for a destination wedding, you may be tempted to have your mother, sister, friend, or other person assist you in the planning process. Intentions are always good, yet things always get complicated when more than one person is calling the shots. To avoid conflict in communication, it is important to designate one person to be fully responsible for making all the decisions. You may also include your loved ones by designating specific tasks indirectly related to the wedding itself. This way you have a direct handle on and are accountable for all of the long-distance services you order. Taking care of rehearsal dinners, group activities, travel arrangements, bridal luncheons, spa days, or shopping excursions is a wonderful way for a loved one to help out.

10 planning basics

1. **Create your wedding wish list with your fiancé.** It is extremely important to determine what you both want prior to diving into the planning process. Size, style or theme, location (on the beach, in a garden, under water . . .) are just a few of the decisions you'll have to make. Don't forget to include the "must haves" and "no ways" on the list.

2. **Set the date.** When getting married in a faraway location, try to select a month first. After the month is selected it's helpful to be flexible when choosing the exact day. I recommend choosing three days (in order of preference) so that you have a number of options available to you.

3. **Create a budget.** Be realistic and don't forget to calculate things like the rings, wedding dress, accessories, travel, accommodations, and honeymoon. Establish an allowance for each item and set aside extra funds for those unexpected luxuries.

4. **Assemble a guest list.** Be selective! Inviting the closest of family and friends allows the wedding to be more intimate. However, keep in mind that on average only about 40 percent of all invitees attend a destination wedding.

5. **Get organized.** A computer is an excellent way to create a database, keep track of your guest list, and create a budget, and it is very useful when doing seating arrangements for the reception. In conjunction with a computer, start a binder with colorful tabs listing every aspect of your wedding. Tabs can include Travel, Accommodations, Locations, Videography and Photography,

Flowers, Wedding Attire, Catering, Entertainment, and Vendors. Create sections where you can gather a collection of cutouts from magazines that represent all your favorite ideas—flowers, wedding music selections, or anything else you might like to incorporate on your wedding day. Your fiancé will get more involved with your ideas, and taking it with you wherever you go makes planning fun.

6. **Choose your island.** Maui, Kaua'i, and Lana'i each have their unique charms. More research may be necessary for you to choose and the Hawai'i Visitors Bureau is a great resource (visit www.gohawaii.com). Once you select your island you can target professionals in that area.

7. **Do your research and decide whether or not to enlist the help of a professional (see page 196).** Make some calls, check references, get referrals. Make sure that the person you select is capable of taking you step by step through the planning process. Once you hire a professional, trust them do what you've hired them to do. This way you will have time to carry out other responsibilities, like finding the perfect wedding dress and all the accessories that go with it, selecting the attire for the groom and wedding parties, writing or customizing the ceremony, planning the engagement party and rehearsal party, registering for gifts, selecting and assembling favors, and going through tons of magazines to get ideas that will help you design your signature event.

8. **Send out save the date cards.** These tell everyone that you're getting married in Hawai'i and give them notice that they should save the date on their calendars if they wish to start planning their trip. I've seen brides-to-be use postcards from Hawai'i, mailable coconuts, and a message in a bottle. You can also create your own cards with tropical designs. Formal invitations can

be sent out at a later date. For destination weddings I recommend sending out a formal invitation three months in advance. Other resources like maps, accommodation information, travel options, and activities are thoughtful things to include with your wedding invitations.

9. **Trust your decisions.** The destination you've selected, the professionals you've hired, and all of the other choices you've made are a representation of who you are. Believe in yourself enough to know that you are making the right choices along the way. Reviewing the final confirmation letter from your wedding coordinator and going over other written documentation you've received prior to setting everything in stone will help calm your pre-wedding jitters so that you can rest assured that your wedding day will be everything that you've dreamed it to be, and more.

10. **Enjoy the moment.** Remember that nothing else matters but the happiness and joy of the two of you uniting together. If there are subtle deviations from the overall plan during your wedding day, chances are that you will be the only one who notices. And if something does happen to go way off track, the best and perhaps only way to handle it is with a smile. Be strong and allow yourselves to enjoy the moment. This is what it's all about.

hiring a wedding coordinator

A successful collaboration with a wedding coordinator can help ensure that you will happily recall your wedding day for years to come. There are many decisions to be made, plans to work out, and responsibilities to delegate. Finding a professional wedding coordinator early in the process gives you an edge in booking locations, securing the best vendors, and getting a handle on hundreds of details. This makes the planning process a lot easier for everyone involved.

Reputable destination wedding coordinators are experienced in working long-distance with clients, and because they consistently hire other professionals in the field, they are quite efficient. In addition, they are experienced in negotiating venues, banquets, and vendor contracts, and can often obtain special discounts that you wouldn't get otherwise. They can anticipate problems, prevent mishaps from affecting your day, and keep you supremely unaware of any troubles. Acting as an extension of you as they confirm your vendors' services, they're fully capable of implementing the most elaborate of details and are in constant communication with the vendors, making sure that nothing gets overlooked. Afterward, they can make sure that the cleanup is competently handled, settle any last-minute charges, and make sure that everyone is taken care of.

When interviewing coordinators, ask them for references and make the calls. Ask your prospective coordinator what the on-site services include on the day of your event and what the payment options are. Most importantly, choose someone whom you connect with, who understands your style, and whom you can trust. Finally, don't be tempted to hire the least expensive coordinator because with quality comes a cost.

things to consider

• Do they carry liability insurance? This is necessary to gain access to the top locations, vendors, and services, and it is required at certain venues. Their having insurance also eliminates the need to purchase it yourself.

• Do they have an official business location?

• How many employees do they have?

• Do they have at least two or three references?

• Is correspondence unlimited?

• Will they return phone calls and e-mails in a timely manner?

• Do they "double up" on services? For example: your musician may offer to take photos for you, your caterer may offer to plan the event for you, your wedding planner may also want to be your musician. You may save a little money, but the quality will suffer. Stick with a professional that specializes in one thing.

• How do they select their vendors? Do they have a pre-selected group of people or do they provide you with all the options available and give helpful advice so that you can make an educated decision?

basic guideline: what a reputable planner's fees should include

PRE-WEDDING DAY COORDINATION

- Allows unlimited correspondence by phone and e-mail.

- Provides information about locations and vendors, gives advice, and makes reservations.

- Secures vendors and handles contracts (officiant, photographer, videographer, florist, musician, and so on).

- Obtains quotes for custom requests.

- Provides information and insight to activites and accomodations.

- Handles all payments and submits necessary deposits.

- Provides a package that includes a confirmation letter with cost itemization and vendor details.

- Arranges the timing and details of each service (vendor arrival times, delivery schedules, and so on).

- Creates a timeline or flow sheet for the couple to use as a guide on their special day.

- Reconfirms all services and takes full responsibility for all vendors secured through the coordinator.

- Carries liability insurance.

ON-SITE COORDINATION

- Directs the flow of events.

- Oversees all vendors hired.

- Meets and greets you and your guests.

- Distributes and pins on all flowers (bouquets, boutonnieres, corsages, leis) ordered by the coordinator.

- Ensures proper setup of décor.

- Carries out the timeline previously established.

- Resolves any unforeseen issues behind the scenes.

ITEMS INCURRING EXTRA FEES AND CUSTOM QUOTES

- Site visits.

- Trial runs, cake tasting, etc. . . .

- Rehearsals.

- On-site coordinating or setting up of *any* items you solely provide (flowers, favors, place cards, and so on).

- Coordinating non-wedding-day events such as welcome receptions or rehearsal dinners.

- Coordinating the reception.

destination wedding timeline

SIX MONTHS TO ONE YEAR BEFORE THE WEDDING

- Start determining your style! Write down each of your wedding wishes.

- Set a date.

- Decide if you want a bridal party; select and ask the persons you've chosen.

- Assemble the guest list.

- Create a budget.

- Get organized (start a binder).

- Select your destination island.

- Decide whether you would like to hire a planner (if so, interview planners and hire one before you do anything else).

- Discuss and determine your wedding location with your planner or start the process on your own if no planner's involved (and secure it).

- Start researching vendors for the ceremony as soon as possible and secure them, or have your planner walk you through the process.

- Research airfare and accommodations.

- Send out save the date cards.

- Go shopping! Select rings and decide on color scheme; select your wedding dress and attire.

- Sign up for gift registry.

THREE TO SIX MONTHS BEFORE THE WEDDING

- Order wedding invitations, announcements, custom stationery, thank-you cards.

- Send out wedding invitations (three months before).

- Create a check list or go over detailed itemization provided by your planner.

- Finalize airfare if you haven't already done so (three months before).

- Finalize accommodations if you haven't already done so.

- Schedule a marriage license appointment on the day before (if you haven't hired a planner).

- Decide on what colors you want for the bridal bouquet.

- Visit a floral shop, go through magazines, and select at least three bouquets (or specific flowers) that you like within your chosen colors and theme.

- Give your color selections and photos to your wedding planner (or selected florist if doing it on your own).

- Secure vendors for ceremony if you're doing it on your own or re-confirm with your planner.

- Research your reception venue and secure the location.

- Discuss and secure specialty items and décor for the ceremony (chairs, floral pathways, floral arrangements, arches, etc.). A planner can be a valuable resource.

- Concentrate on your health and start an exercise routine if you haven't done so already.

continued

destination wedding timeline

- Trust in your decisions.

- Spend time with your sweetheart.

- Cherish your engagement.

ONE TO THREE MONTHS BEFORE THE WEDDING

- Pick up your wedding dress (can ship to a reputable presser at or near your hotel).

- Schedule and have an engagement photo taken (which you also may send with an announcement to the local newspapers).

- Go shopping! Get travel gear, wedding party gifts, and so on.

- Rent tuxedos (if applicable) through planner or on your own.

- Schedule measurement appointments for groomsmen at a reputable shop in their home towns.

- Discuss and secure specialty items and décor for the reception (centerpieces, favors, place cards, and so on).

- Finalize your floral order.

- Finalize reception details.

- Secure transportation for bride and wedding party (if applicable).

- Research and secure reservations for a pre-wedding group activity or rehearsal dinner (if applicable).

ONE WEEK TO ONE MONTH BEFORE THE WEDDING

- Revise and double-check your list of services for the wedding and reception or go over the revised detailed itemization provided by your wedding planner.

- Reconfirm your travel and accommodations (for the honeymoon too).

- Create an itinerary for you and your guests (start from your arrival date) and e-mail or make copies to give to everyone.

- Get your manicure and pedicure done prior to your arrival.

- Start packing and bring wedding information, maps, etc. with you.

- Plan a romantic dinner with your fiancé.

UPON ARRIVAL

- Don't forget to wear sunscreen.

- Pick up tuxedos (if applicable).

- Obtain marriage license.

- Attend prearranged group activity, bridal luncheon, or luau.

- Concentrate on each other, be flexible, and have fun!

destination wedding worksheet

Before you get lost in all your options, try to get an idea of what style you want your destination wedding to be. Here is a worksheet to help the two of you create your vision.

Preferred island: Visit www.gohawaii.com to learn about Hawai'i.

Maui   Kaua'i   Lana'i

Do I want to hire a professional wedding planner?   Yes   No

Guest list: The size of your group will narrow down your location search. This saves you tons of time since your focus will only be on the locations that will accommodate your size group.

2–25   26–50   51–75   76–100   100+

Preferred level of privacy: Determining the level of privacy you prefer will narrow down your location (venue) options. Select one.

Very private   Semiprivate   Public   Doesn't matter

Preferred wedding location: Close your eyes for a moment and try to picture your wedding day. Do you see a garden, beach, or both? Circle two of your favorite options from the list below.

Garden	Beach	Garden and beach
Resort with beach	Waterfall	Remote
Private property/estate	Courthouse	Church
Cliff	Oceanfront	Oceanview

Tip: In the unlikely event that it rains, you may need to plan a backup location. Please go over all of your backup location options with your wedding coordinator or location contact prior to securing the venue. Backup locations can include a ballroom, a covered lanai, a gazebo, a chapel, an indoor/outdoor function area, or an overhang area. Tent options can be explored depending on your venue.

Preferred attire: Determining the kind of attire you prefer will be helpful when creating your budget. Select one (if you choose formal wear, then indicate whether you will need tuxedo rental(s) and dress-pressing services.

Casual wear   Formal wear   Resort wear

Tuxedo rental(s)   Dress-pressing service

Tip: Due to the limited options, I suggest that you get your dress at home and carry it with you on the plane or ship it (via UPS or FedEx) to a reputable dress presser on the island. You can then pick it up after you arrive. Tuxedos can be rented on Maui and Kaua'i. Brides: Do not attempt to measure your man by yourself! Professional measurements assure a comfortable fit, and you will avoid fees incurred because of inaccurate measurements that have been taken by someone who's not familiar with the process. Tuxedo charts can be provided by your wedding planner or tux shop along with the pickup and return procedures.

Preferred emotional elements (setting the mood): Whether you want a traditional or Hawaiian-style wedding, this is where you get to show off your personalities. You can be as creative or as conservative as you want. Here are some popular Island-themed elements. Just keep in mind that the more you select, the more money you need to set aside for this section.

Canoe processional   Chanters

Conch shell blower   Plumeria-lined pathways
                            (seasonal)
Polynesian trio

Native flora   Kahili bearers

Hula dancer   Lei greeter

continued

destination wedding worksheet

Lei exchange during ceremony

Special leis given to parents during ceremony

Bamboo arches

Monarch butterfly release

Hawaiian save the date cards

Island-themed invitations

Tiki torches

Fire knife dancer

Twinkle lights and palm trees

Conch shell centerpieces

Hawaiian-themed favors

Woven centerpieces, flower baskets, and pillows

Free-standing bamboo poles with tropical arrangements sitting on top

Woven mats for children to play on

Hawaiian music with hula dancers or custom luau show

Weavers that weave items on the spot to give to you and your guests

Lei makers that teach lei making

Wood carvers that carve a masterpiece to give to the bride and groom

Shell or nut bracelets as favors or place-card holders

Minister: Please check your officiant preference. Ceremony selections are available upon request once your minister has been confirmed.

Religious   Nonreligious   Specific-faith minister   Doesn't matter

Musicians: There is no better way to set the mood than adding a live musician to perform during your ceremony. Here are your standard selections.

Acoustical guitar   Guitar w/vocals   Harp

Hawaiian ukulele   Flute   Violin

Duo   Trio

Photographers and videographers: Choose what style you're interested in, then choose the amount of coverage time you think you may need. Minimum photo packages start at one hour, and minimum video packages start at two hours. Unless it's a beach wedding with 10 or less guests, I recommend a minimum of 2 hours coverage time. Consider these questions: Do you want pre-location coverage? pre-ceremony coverage of wedding party arriving and getting ready? What about afterward? Do you want coverage of the cake cutting, champagne toast, or reception?

Photography styles

Traditional portraiture   Photojournalistic   Candid

Traditional portraiture w/ photojournalism

Other/Special Requests _____

Videography styles

Home video   Video journalistic   Documentary

Short movie   Other/Special Requests _____

How many hours of coverage do you want?   _____

Flowers: Choosing your flower colors *first* is the most important thing you can do. Then you can select flowers within your color scheme that are easily available to you. After your color scheme is determined, choose the style and size of the bouquet you want.

*Color scheme*_____

Style

   Cascading   Nosegay   French   Arm bouquet

Size

   Extra small   Small   Medium   Large

   Extra large

continued

destination wedding worksheet

Other bridal flowers

Lei exchange for couple   Groom's boutonniere

Corsages (wrist/pin)   Single flowers for hair

Haku head lei   Ankle lei

Groomsmen's boutonnieres/leis   Bridesmaids' flowers/leis

Guest leis   Custom arrangements

Rose petal sprinkle   Floral pathway

Cake and champagne toast   Yes   No

   Single-tier   Two-tier   Two-tier pedastal

Rental Items

Chairs   Arch   Audio services   Columns or urns   Other

Hair and/or makeup

How many to be serviced? _____   In-room   Salon

Transportation

Limo   Sedan   Vans   SUV   Canoe

Other_____

Marriage license: Reservations can be made anytime for an appointment within thirty days prior to your event. I recommend scheduling your appointment the day before your wedding. Maps to and from the licenser's office will be available after your appointment is secured.

Preferred date: _____
Preferred appointment time: a.m. or p.m.

reception planner worksheet

The usual rules change when a couple travels to an exotic location to celebrate their union: finding a reception location should always be secondary. Securing your dream wedding location *first* allows you to focus on the reception venue options nearby, saving you tons of time. Keeping the ceremony and reception close to each other also makes it convenient for your family and friends.

Here are a few "must know" guidelines when it comes to selecting that perfect reception site.

- All venues are subject to availability, and some venues can't be reserved without a signed contract and nonrefundable deposits.

- Some reception locations do not confirm or guarantee space until ninety days prior to wedding date.

- Setup fees and linen-rental fees will apply at all locations.

- A 19–21 percent gratuity will be added to all food and beverage.

- All alcohol must be purchased on-site if you select a restaurant or resort.

- County noise ordinances dictate that all outdoor functions must end by 9 or 10 p.m. (depending on the location).

- Don't expect your prospective venue to give out references.

Budget: I have found that wedding receptions can range from $50 to $200 per person, depending on the venue, menu selections, bar option and type of alcohol served, and décor. I suggest budgeting at least $100 per person (all-inclusive), unless you are going with a restaurant or a modest venue and caterer.

Pre-visits: If you feel the need to fly to the Islands in advance, here are some guidelines and rules of etiquette prior to making your rounds.

- If you are considering hiring an event planner, then conduct these interviews first. This will give the planner greater control to do what you are hiring them to do.

- It is your responsibility to inform site providers if you're planning the wedding on your own, if you've hired a wedding planner (and who that is), or if you plan on working with a planner. This will avoid any awkwardness and miscommunication with the site provider.

- Be prepared to pay prospective vendors—including stylists, musicians, and pastry chefs (to name a few)—their regular fees if you wish to do a trial run at any time prior to your event.

Money-saving tips: The only way to save is to keep it simple. Don't get caught up in a lot of details, allow the venue itself to be your décor, have your guests pay for their own alcohol, and be flexible with your menu. Designate guests to be responsible for specific tasks like setting place cards and favors.

Quotes: Your planner, restaurant, caterer, or resort should be able to give you a detailed cost itemization prior to the event so that you can see what the total charges will be. Some locations will require some or all of it up-front. A reputable planner is your best bet for delivering accurate information to you prior to the event with no surprises or hidden fees afterwards. I have often found errors in bills, so reviewing them closely ensures accuracy.

Setup: Request a floor plan so that you can get a detailed idea on where your tables will be in relation to your musicians, sign-in table, cake display, and buffet. Linen options, chair options, centerpieces, and lighting can be discussed at this time. You can also determine if you want open seating or place-card seating. For the latter, you will have to provide a seating chart with the cards and a person responsible for setting this up, unless you pay an additional fee to your planner or site provider to handle this for you.

reception planner worksheet

Fill out this questionnaire prior to selecting your reception venue:

Do you want an indoor or outdoor reception?

Indoor (no music curfews)   Outdoor (9 or 10 p.m. music curfew)

Would you prefer a restaurant or more private venue?

Resort   Restaurant   Private venue

Guest list:

2–25   26–50   51–75   76–100   100+

Do you want to provide appetizers (pupus) during your cocktail hour?

Yes   No

Preference of cuisine?

American   Hawaiian   Asian   Italian   Seafood   other

Would you like wedding cake to be served in place of your desserts or do you want to offer both?

Cake   Desserts   Both

What bar option would you like to provide (private venues only)? The choices are on-consumption (pay afterwards on what's consumed), full bar (pre-pay per person by the hour), and cash bar (guests pay a cashier for their drinks). Bartender and cashier fees may apply with any of the options.

On-consumption   Full bar   Cash bar

reception planner worksheet

Do you want to provide a champagne toast or signature drink? (One bottle of champagne fills five glasses.)

Champagne toast   Signature drink

Live music or DJ?

Live   DJ

Would you like to include any Hawaiian entertainment (hula dancers, fire knife, Polynesian trio, other)?

Yes   No

Do you want to include dancing for you and your guests?

Yes   No

Special requests?

Flower arrangements   Ice sculptures   Rose petal sprinkle

Tiki torches   Twinkle lights   Hawaiian-themed items

Other site considerations: Please don't let the menu, lighting, music, bar arrangements, setup, and other details get in the way when selecting that perfect site. Most of those details can be worked out later. Instead, ask yourself, Does it feel right? Will it accommodate your guests? What are the site fee(s)? Will you have to bring in a caterer or rent tables, chairs, plateware, and so on? Are there any restrictions to the venue? What is the music curfew? Is it required that you work with specific vendors? Transportation and parking are other matters. You may need to hire group transportation ensure access to parking.

reception planner worksheet

basic budget worksheet

Determining your budget will help you when selecting which items you may need to forgo. Your wedding coordinator can provide you with a detailed itemization of costs for services on island. If you're doing it on your own, then you will need to get quotes on specific services from the vendors you are considering. Here is a list of items you will need to consider when creating your budget. The average couple spends approximately $25,000 for their wedding.

Before you arrive

Travel   _____

Airfare   _____

Accommodations   _____

Car rental   _____

Attire

Rings   _____

Bride's dress   _____

Groom's wear/tuxedo   _____

Bridal party wear
(include flower girl and ring bearer w/accessories)   _____

Bridal accessories (jewelry, shoes, etc.)   _____

Groom's accessories (cufflinks, etc.)   _____

Beauty

Pre-wedding haircut and a trial up-do for bride   _____
(with current beautician)

New waterproof makeup   _____

Pre-wedding manicure and pedicure   _____

Groom's services   _____

Other (perfume, cologne, etc.)   _____

Stationery

Save the date cards   _____

Invitations   _____

Calligraphy service   _____

Announcements   _____

Thank-you cards   _____

Postage   _____

Specialty stationery   _____

Destination wedding services

Wedding coordinator   _____

Wedding grounds fee

Reception grounds fee   _____

Marriage license   _____

Rehearsal dinner (if applicable)   _____

Bridal luncheon (optional)   _____

Spa treatment or massage   _____

Tuxedo rental   _____

Activities   _____

Other   _____

Day of wedding

Minister   _____

Musician   _____

Photographer   _____

Videographer   _____

continued

basic budget worksheet

Flowers, pathways
(in general your flowers will cost more in Hawai'i
than on the mainland, especially those difficult-to-get flowers)   _____

Arch, chairs, other rental items
(include setup, delivery, and removal)   _____

Elements and custom décor   _____

Day-of-event hair and makeup service   _____

Cake   _____

Champagne toast   _____

Sparkling apple cider   _____

Custom wedding certificate   _____

Special transportation for bride's arrival   _____

Special transportation for bride
and groom's departure   _____

Group transportation to and from wedding
and reception   _____

Tax   _____

Gratuities   _____

Miscellaneous/special services   _____

Other considerations

Engagement party   _____

Favors   _____

Special gifts for selected individuals   _____

Daily spending cash for bride and
groom while on island   _____

Reception   _____

Honeymoon   _____

Miscellaneous   _____

❧ basic budget worksheet

a final note

I hope you have found this guide useful and I value your input. Please visit www.hawaiiweddingbook.com or e-mail truelove@maui.net to share your feedback and wedding experiences.

Overall, just remember to take one step at a time, have fun, and most importantly, never lose sight of what brought you and your love together. Congratulations and happy planning.

acknowledgments

I would like to dedicate this book to my dear friend Sarah A. K. Makua. She worked many days and sacrificed much of her time writing location descriptions, all because she believed in me and this project. Without her genuine support and relentless efforts this book would not exist.

Sarah, I couldn't have done it without you. Your friendship means more to me than you could ever imagine. How can I ever thank you enough for all you have done? I hope you know how much I love you.

To my loving husband, Todd Perkins, and my beautiful daughter, Melanie Ash, I am deeply grateful for your loving presence. Thank you for your endless support. I would also like to acknowledge my dear friend Robin Liska, my colleagues and friends Debbie Graham and Victoria Joyce, my dedicated staff Marla Tanouye and Tamorro Farrell, my wonderful editor Alma Bune, and publisher Karen Bouris. Your inspiration and encouragement can be found within the pages of this book, and I thank you all from the bottom of my heart.

I would like to send a special thank you to my Mom, Diane Chipperfield. *Mom, I can't tell you how much I deeply appreciate your unconditional love and support. You have always been there for me and for that I will be forever grateful. I love you Mom!*

I would like to express my gratitude to the many photographers who so graciously contributed their photos. I am honored to have such a fine team of professionals supporting me on this project. I will cherish your friendship always. Mahalo nui loa!

And finally, to all of those who have chosen Hawai'i as your wedding location and to the professionals and friends in the field who have supported me and continue to do so. You truly are the ones that have inspired me to write this book. Thank you, thank you, thank you!

about the author

Originally from Colorado, **Tammy Perkins** has made Hawai'i her home since 1992. She founded First Class Weddings, Inc. (www.firstclass-weddings.com) in 1994 and has since planned thousands of weddings. She was honored with the "Women Who Mean Business" award given to the top 25 women-owned businesses by *Pacific Business News* and has featured a wedding on The Travel Channel. She is a member of the Better Business Bureau, and as a board member of Maui Youth and Family Services (MYFS), she currently helps raise funds for the nonprofit agency in support of the organization's mission to help build better lives for Hawai'i's families. She lives on Maui with her husband, Todd, and 16 year-old daughter, Melanie.

index

notes

notes

notes

notes

notes

notes

notes

– notes – Jasmine

– Christine –

Westin – 6 sites 750-2000
Boardwalk Lawn – 1.000
ocean front – 10 steps – 1.000
from Beach

pkgs – $1,100   2ND tier $1,900
cake/champagne
non-dominational
officient
lei's
coordinatn

Top left: Makena Cove,
Maui © Mike Sydney;
right: Kapalua Bay
Beach, Maui © A&C
Photography; *bottom:*
Kalihiwai Bay, Kaua'i
© Sarah Makua

Top: Ka'anapali Beach, Maui © Mike Sydney; *bottom left*: Kapalua Bay Beach, Maui © Pete Thompson; *right*: Po'olenalena Beach, Maui © A&C Photography

Top left: Ka'anapali Beach, Maui © Λ&C Photography; *right:* Po'olenalena Beach, Maui © Mike Sydney; *bottom:* Ironwood Beach, Maui © Pete Thompson

Top: Grand Wailea
Seaside Chapel, Maui
© Mike Sydney;
bottom left: Maria
Lanakila Church, Maui
© A&C Photography;
right: From inside St.
John's Church, Maui
© Pete Thompson

Top: St John's Church, Maui; *middle:* Honolua Chapel, Maui; *bottom:* Sacred Hearts Church, Maui. All photos © Pete Thompson

Top: Four Seasons
Resort, Maui © Bill
Stockwell; *bottom:*
Moir Gardens, Kaua'i
© Sarah Makua

Top left: Grand Wailea
Resort gazebo, Maui
© A&C Photography;
right: Ritz-Carlton
Kapalua, Maui © Bill
Stockwell; *bottom*:
Upper courtyard of
Maui Prince Hotel,
Maui © Mike Sydney

Top left: Fairmont Kea Lani gazebo, Maui; *right:* Fairmont Kea Lani 6th floor alcove; *bottom:* Hyatt Regency Maui Resort statue gardens. All photos © A&C Photography

Top: Ritz-Carlton
Kapalua gazebo, Maui
© Pete Thompson;
left and right: Grand
Wailea, Maui © A&C
Photography

Top: © Mike Sydney;
middle: © Mike
Andrews; *bottom left
and right:* © A&C
Photography

Top left and right:
© A&C Photography;
bottom: © MauiFoto
Photography

Photography by Bill Stockwell

www.billstockwell.com

email awareguy@aol.com

phone 808 879 7200

*F*or your special day on *Maui*, we offer a treasure of motion and sound to enjoy for years to come. We use a photojournalistic and an unobtrusive style to capture your personal love story on DVD or VHS tape.

Surefire
PRODUCTIONS

1-808-874-8230
info@surefireproductions.com
www.surefireproductions.com